It's All In Your Mind

By Noel Cox

"A life of mediocrity is the price one pays for failing to use the imagination"

It's All In Your Mind

Printed by arrangement with

www.MagusMind.com

Our goal is your Higher Potential

Contact: info@magusmind.com

A leading online resource for the products, learning and practice of the science of personal development and helping people reach their higher potential.

First Trade Paperback Edition 2004

Copyright 2004 by Noel Cox

ISBN 1-4116-1482-8

It's All In Your Mind

This book is dedicated to Michael and Olive, the best parents I could ever
have asked for. May the light you started shine the way to a brighter future
for many. Also, to my wonderful wife, Carmen, your love and kindness have
been a source of joy and inspiration. I am blessed to have met you. I also
dedicate this book to YOU, may you find the truth about the higher potential
that awaits your discovery within you.

It's All In Your Mind

Acknowledgement

I wish to express my gratitude to Sean and Helen of Rapidmultimedia.com for their loving support. Your professionalism and balanced feedback have been appreciated greatly, and you have helped make MagusMind.com become a reality. I also wish to thank my brother, Brian, your support and faith in me has been an inspiration and I am proud of the man you are.

It's All In Your Mind

It's All In Your Mind

Contents

Introduction   8

Section 1

Gaining Control of Your Mind and Your Life.

Simplify Your Life   12

Take Control of Your Environment   16

Take Responsibility and Take Control.   21

Make Your Vocation Your Vacation   23

The Power of Decisions   24

Self-Concept   26

Inferiority Complex   29

The Trip Switch Technique for Changing

Negative Self-talk Into Positive Living.   35

Recreate Your Own Empowering Memories.   40

Pain and Pleasure Principle   42

Stress and Anxiety   44

Sponsoring Image and Trigger Words Technique.   54

The Power Walk.   56

Creating Your Own Inner Sanctuary to

Overcome Fear and Panic.   58

Habits – The tracks of Rabbits   59

The Importance of Imagination.   61

Improve Your Senses and Get More Out of Life.   64

A Change in Perception   67

The Power of Love and Passion.   69

The Importance of Forgiveness.   75

It's All In Your Mind

Understanding   77
Communication   78
Smile and the Whole World Smiles With You.   85
The Secret of Living is Giving   87

Section 2

Harnessing the Hidden Power In Your Mind
The Power of Focus and Concentration.   89
Affirmations and Visualisations   94
The Secret Path To Success   98
Know What You Want, Setting Goals and the Success Collage 100
Desire it Hard Enough   110
Have Faith, Belief and Expectancy that It Will Happen. 114
Belief and the Placebo Effect   118
Be Persistent Towards Its Attainment and
Learn From Your Outcomes   122
Be Willing To Pay the Price   124
Be Do Have your Way to Happiness and Success   126
Use Your Subconscious Intuition to Solve Problems   130
The 10 Steps to Scientific Prayer.   131

Section 3

Relaxation and The Mind Studio Method   134
Relax and Breathe Your Way to Maximum Well-being.   137
Progressive Relaxation   141

Your Personal Mind Counsellors 147

The Mind Studio 150

Applications of the Mind Studio 156

A Final Word 167

Recommendations 168

Recommended Reading List 170

It's All In Your Mind

Introduction

Dear Friend,

It's All In Your Mind, how often we have heard this statement. When we were kids and ran in fear of the closet monster we were told, "it's all in your mind." The truth is that everything in your life is all in your mind. Your thoughts, your fears, your desires, your loves and hates, your successes, your failings, and your circumstances are All In Your Mind. You are about to embark on a journey into the inner workings of your mind, and by the time you place this book down, you will have the tools and mental techniques to help you have anything you could want in life. The purpose of this book is not to tell you how to live your live, but rather to provide you with the mental skills that will help you tap the hidden springs of your mind and to live the life of your desire. I have always been intrigued as to what made one person reach great heights of achievement and tremendous success, while others lead a sleepwalking type of existence constantly in a state of worry and bad health, never finding true contentment. What makes those other people have boundless energy, health, wealth and happiness? How come they seem to achieve so much against all kinds of odds, and in such short periods of time, while others seem to work hard yet never get anywhere?

These are the questions that burned in my mind and I began to read voraciously to seek the answers. I read hundreds of books on psychology, spiritualism, and Eastern philosophy and travelled to many countries around the world in search of the key to reaching our higher potential. What I found is that truth really is stranger than fiction and that we have unlimited potential as human beings. We use only a minute amount of our mental capacity, and we are only beginning to learn of the fantastic potential that lies within the human mind. I have come to realize that thoughts are things and that you and everything in your life are the result of the thoughts that occupy your mind. Once you learn the secrets of your mind, you will be able to have anything you could want in your life. It could be financial independence, a loving relationship, a closer relationship to God, true contentment whatever it may be, know that you can have and achieve it. Nature does not plant the seed of a desire in a human, without also providing the means and potential of achieving it.

It still baffles me to this day that our so called education system, which is supposed to prepare us for life does not at any point teach the young child how to do the most fundamental things that are paramount to success such as, how to set goals, how to handle rejection and control fears, how to better make decisions, how to use their own mind to their greater benefit and not against them. I believe that every individual has special talents, and all they have to do is learn how to seek them out and claim their divine right to greater happiness and love. Unfulfilled potential is truly one of the greatest shames. I endeavour to present these ideas and methods in as clear and concise a way as possible. It is essentially a course in taking you from wherever you may be at the current time, and helping you reach your higher potential. I say a course, because I urge you to not merely read the book passively, but to *do* the exercises and repeat them until you achieve results. Action is what unites the spiritual with the physical. Much of what has been written has been condensed down and distilled to its simplest and purest form. This book could easily have been three times its size, however I endeavoured to present the ideas to you without the psychology jargon or dressed up language. Please do not be put off by the simplicity of the various techniques mentioned in the book, and I ask that you read each section carefully so as not to overlook the little psychological gems that exist in each part. May I also at this point advise that much of what is written in this book focuses on the power of your mind and drawing out its potential. I am working under the assumption that you are taking steps to take care of your health in all aspects of your life, including the foods you eat and your exercise habits. I shall not be dealing with the area of diet or physical fitness in this body of work, and urge you to research all that you can in these areas. A healthy body leads to a healthy mind, and most importantly a healthy mind leads to a healthy body. Much of the effectiveness of the techniques in this work can be hampered if you do not take care in your diet, and maintain a good level of physical fitness. The course starts off with gaining perspective on life and how to first of all gain direction and take control of your mind. It is said that you feel happy to the degree you feel in control of your life and circumstances. Well, that is one of our first objectives for you to gain control of your life and to find that direction. Together we shall clear that mist and shine a light on the path to your highest potential. The later chapters shall deal with creating true magic in your life. I understand that some of the techniques may seem a bit strange at first, and trust me I was a sceptic too, but once I began to apply what I had learned, they took me places I never imagined I would be and provided me with the tools to thrive in the face of any challenge I was met with. I request that you suspend judgement for a time and simply try them. The concepts in this book shall do different things for different people. For some, this book will help them gain more confidence and to live their life more effectively in the absence of that constant state of fear and anxiety. Others shall find their soul mates and some will go on to live a life of pure magic and wonder.

It is my understanding that everyone wants to feel better. That is why coffee shops are so prolific in society. People go there to buy something that will make them feel better. The unfortunate thing is that it is short lasting and has after effects on the body and mind. There are more lasting ways to feeling better and they shall be presented in this book. A coffee high without the Caffeine! There are few subjects that will reward you and enrich your life as much the science of mind and spirit, and I do not by any means claim to be an expert on the field. I am a perpetual student of the principles and simply would like to share with you the techniques and principles that I have found to be truly effective in bringing about positive change in my life. The only limits to what you can achieve are those that you acknowledge, so let us begin to knock down the barriers and to bring you all that you desire by discovering the magic in your mind.

Noel Cox.

Section 1
Gaining Control of Your Mind and Your Life.

Simplify Your Life -The Mental Audit

One of the most liberating things you can do is to simplify your life by reducing the things that bring you pain and increasing the activities that give you pleasure. By doing so you will find that your peace of mind and happiness increase almost straight away. Take stock of the amount of activities that fill your week. How many obligations have you allowed yourself to be committed to, but really in the back of your mind you would rather do something else. A hectic schedule without any time for relaxation indicates that you may not have had the confidence to say no to something or certain people in your life when you really would have preferred you had. If you find yourself with little time to relax and do the things that you would really like to do then it is an indication that you need to do a little mental stock taking, assert yourself more and audit your time more effectively. As odd as it seems many of us do not feel comfortable with ourselves. We may find it excruciating to sit alone in silence and are infinitely creative in finding ways to avoid such a travesty. It is the very opposite that we should be striving to do. You may find that you fill every spare moment of your day and your week with many activities that you simply do not enjoy and certainly don't inspire you. Are you one of those people that always seem to be run off your feet and flying from task to task, and never seem to be making any progress? It's as if nature has placed a treadmill under your feet and the faster you go, the less you seem to be able to keep up. Stop for a moment and take stock of how you manage your time. Be more assertive in your decisions about how you wish to spend your valuable time. So, if you really would like to take that walk by the ocean on Wednesday night instead of going to that event or club to which you were reluctantly dragged into, then resolve to do it. Learn to say no to the things that you really do not desire to do, and understand it is your right to choose what you do as an individual. Be aware of emotional blackmail, and realize that it holds no power over you in the moment that you decide not to allow it to effect you or make you feel guilty. You cannot be made to feel guilty or sad or happy without your permission. What I mean is that when you are subjected to an emotional assault from another because you will not do the thing that they want you to do, then how you respond to that is completely your responsibility. If someone insults you, you can choose how to respond to that internally. If someone calls you an unpleasant name you may find yourself getting upset. The truth is that you have chosen to allow yourself to be upset by your interpretation of what was said. This leaves you vulnerable to the behaviour and attitudes of others, because you are so caught up with impressing them with your need for social acceptance as a human being that you remain at the whim of their every comment. Thus you become obsessive about protecting the ego at all costs. That is why, we remain in certain situations that stifle the very life force from us, because we believe that if we stop and attempt to do something else, that we may be met with disapproval from the people that we desire to maintain social bonds with. The best way to impress others is by *not* trying to impress them. You must focus on impressing yourself first before you can impress others. You must look inward if you are to achieve desirable conditions in your outward life.

It's All In Your Mind

As within, so without. It's quite common that by shear force of habit, guilt
and our desire to please others, that we allow ourselves to become emotional
slaves and remain in circumstances that really do not inspire us. Now let's
be clear here, I'm not talking about walking away from all responsibilities
and commitments, but rather that you strive for more balance in your life.
Clear the mist and clutter from your mind and do the things that you truly
would like to do, and not what others think you ought to do. Conduct an
audit of your time and activities.   You may start by making a list of the
things that take up your time during the day and evening. Include on your
list the things that you will be doing over the next week or month. This will
also be a useful list if your conditions are the opposite to what has just been
discussed and you may actually find that you don't do anything at all with
your spare time.   In that instance it will help you identify areas of
opportunity to inject more excitement and enjoyment into your life.

Rate each item on your list on a scale of 1-10 on how much pleasure you
derive from each activity. 1 indicating that you really do not enjoy that
activity at all, 5 being a relatively pleasurable experience, and right up to a
whopping experience of 10. This will give you an idea of how much of your
time is spent on various activities and how much enjoyment you are
experiencing.

Your goal now is to identify items on your list that are rated below 5 and ask
yourself the following questions;

1. How may I improve on this experience and make it as close to 10 as
   possible?

And/or

2. What can I replace this activity with that will bring me far more pleasure and enjoyment in my life?

Brainstorm with a pen and paper and write down the things that you could imagine spending this time doing that would excite you and inspire you. Just jot down the ideas, and don't restrict yourself. Don't pass any judgement on the ideas that arrive simply place them down on paper. Once you have your list. Read over them again. They should be inspiring and exciting enough to instil a strong sense of desire in you. If not review your list and add some more exciting items, things that you would truly like to be doing. The idea of this exercise is to free up more of your time and to simplify your life to a point were you are back in full control, rather than running on a perpetual autopilot. Those that do this simple exercise often find that it they end up with not only more guilt free time on their hands, but also injecting much needed pleasure in their lives. I like to free up time for reading, and meditation, and found the above exercise liberating and empowering.

It's All In Your Mind

Take Control of Your Environment.

Anyone who has ever watched a stage hypnotist operate will realize that we are very impressionable creatures. The subject obeys every instruction given by the hypnotist, and acts in ways that he or she may not otherwise act. We are subjected to similar suggestions in our environment all the time. That is why the large corporations spend huge sums on advertising. From the moment you wake up in the morning you are receiving information at a level which is suggestible to your mind, whether you know it or not. I recommend that you seriously take stock of what you allow into the gateway of your mind on a daily basis and how it affects your life. Our mind may be likened to a sponge that soaks up information that we receive through our sensory organs. A typical scenario may be that you awake in the morning to the sound of an alarm and then open your eyes with dread. The internal voice greets you with, "Oh no, not another day…what I wouldn't give for one more hour of sleep," or something to that effect. Then upon arising you may switch on the news on the radio and hear all about the negative things going on in the world as your first thoughts in the morning. By the way the news is seldom about the positive aspects of society and clearly focuses on all the bad things that occur. So not only have you heard yourself dread the day, but you've also subjected yourself to the world's woes, all before having breakfast.

During our waking consciousness we have varying degrees of wakefulness. We operate at different brain wave patterns during the day. Before going to bed and upon arising in the morning you're generally operating in the relaxed state. This is one of our healthiest states to be in, a kind of relaxed alertness. However, at a relaxed state we are at our most suggestible and receptive to outside images, sounds, smells and feelings. I would like you to be mindful of how you are literally programming your mind with the messages you allow into your environment. Be more discerning about what you allow yourself to focus your attention on at any given time. A good place to start is the walls of your bedroom. Note what posters, pictures you have on your wall or on those of your children if you have them. In the relaxed state in the morning your eyes will settle on a suggestible image such as a poster and note it's very details in the back of your mind. I find it daunting to see some of the posters that people allow their kids to have in their bedrooms. Some are strewn with Heavy Metal images of death and messages of an incredibly negative nature. The mind is impressionable to these messages and although a child may not obviously do anything heinous based on that alone, it does not do the mental well-being of the individual any good at all. As will be explained in later sections, like thoughts attract to themselves other similar thoughts.

Have you ever heard a song first thing in the morning and then not been able to get it out of your mind until late that night, even songs that you do not like? That is symptomatic of the relaxed state programming and runs through your mind all day long even while doing other tasks. In addition to being aware of how the visual images impact on your thoughts, also be aware of how the lyrics of songs can impact your moods or thought patterns. It is worth pointing out that our thought patterns are like the branches of a tree and once you focus your mind on a certain idea, it attracts to it other like thoughts and all are connected via a string of associations. We can see evidence of this in our communication too. You may enjoy demonstrating this to yourself in conversations with others. All you have to do is mention a situation or idea during a conversation, and then watch how the idea spawns among the group. Like a seed dropped in fertile soil it will germinate and grow within the minds of the participants. You will note that for the next ten minutes all people in the group will continue to discuss are like minded issues for a good deal of time. This is the magnetic force of thought, in that each thought entertained in the mind attracts to it other similar thoughts. Your job in reaching your goal of gaining back the self control of your mind is to be more discerning as to what you allow yourself to focus on. All you have to do is pay attention to some of the lyrics of songs and note how destructive they are. Many focus on depending on others, or how their life will fall apart if someone leaves them. What this does is reduce a person's capacity to be independent and fosters the dependency syndrome, whereby someone feels that they cannot live without another. I'm all for passion, but I'm also for people being emotionally strong enough to stand on their own two feet when situations change. So, enjoy the magic of music and it's mood-altering effects, by all means, but be an educated listener and let the messages you hear be ones that you are aware of and consent too. I have always listened to all kinds of music and only when I became fully aware of the way these messages were creating impressions on my mind did I begin to filter out certain damaging songs. There is a magical property in music and you always have a choice of what kinds you listen to.

It goes without saying that this extends to our conversations with others. Have you ever met someone who constantly harps on about the difficulties of life and indeed how they are so hard done by the system the government and everyone from the president to the butcher? We all know people like this, and after talking with them you feel a heck of a lot worse than you did before encountering them. Do not get caught up in this kind of conversation and allow yourself to take on the same negative thought patterns. They are literally energy vampires and drain you of any positivity that you may have had left after the posters, the news, and the negative self-talk. There is a simple method of protecting yourself from this energy drain,

Imagine yourself contained inside an energy bubble. It extends all around you. This may be likened to a see through egg. In your mind imagine that this shields all negativity from reaching you. Imagine the words of the person simply bouncing off the edges of the energy bubble and dissipating in the atmosphere.

That which you focus on grows. So when you create this energy force field around your body often it will grow in strength and protect you from the energy drain.

Consciously remind yourself that you reject negative talk. If you find yourself saying something negative along with the other, in your inner voice say

"Delete that message."

It is also quite important to remain in a nurturing positive encouraging environment. We all know the effects of spending time with people who harbour negative or destructive states of mind. If we are not careful the very force of their negative emotions can surround you and penetrate your mind and before you know it you shall be resonating the same thoughts, feelings and behaviours as the people in your environment. This comes about through the same principle that the sounding of a tuning fork can resonate the corresponding wires in a piano or on a guitar. Spend as much time in the environments and places that are consistent with the life that you want. Think carefully about the kinds of people that you associate with and be aware of the influence that their thoughts and attitudes have on you. You can protect yourself from the negative thoughts of others by mentally saying to yourself, "I am a strong courageous being and you have no power over me. I deny you any influence over me, " and direct this thought to the people while you hold a conversation with them. This will give you a sense of control and help you repel the negative energy that is blasted at you in waves from people suffering from a bad outlook on life. It is in this way that a student in a class of achievers is carried on a wave of enthusiasm, belief and positive expectancy when in a class of talented and ambitious individuals. It goes without saying that the opposite is the case in a class of individuals who have no drive or ambitions whatsoever. It takes a great will indeed to rise above this group when bathed daily in the quagmire of their lack of drive or desire for anything worthwhile. That is not to say that there is no hope for the latter, all they need is their desire and will stirred to a degree as to cause them to positively believe themselves to be something better to go after that which they desire.

It's All In Your Mind

Take Responsibility Take Control.

One of the most empowering truths that I came across at an early stage is that *we are all responsible for our own lives.* Once this truth is understood, the bonds and chains that have been placed on us by ourselves begin to weaken and fall away. No matter what your circumstance you have the power to choose. Too many people live their lives allowing and asking others to make decisions for them. From an early stage in our development, we depend on our parents to make decisions for us. Then for much of our youth we rely on others for our life's necessities and very seldom make great decisions of our own initiative. Very often after finishing school and entering the world of work we have not reached a signpost that states, now is the time for you to take responsibility for your own decisions and life. Instead many simply transfer the paternal decision-making responsibility to someone else. They may not feel capable of making real decisions by themselves. So they give the responsibility to others, who may be a partner or a boss or friend or whomever. What this results in is a situation where someone else is always in control of your decisions and hence your life. It is a reality that;

If you do not make the important decisions in your life, then others will make them for you.

You will never have a real sense of control so long as you default your decisions to someone else. Stop crowning someone else in the kingdom of your life. It is you that is the heir and the king or Queen of your circumstances. It is fine to respect and admire people, but is it healthy to place someone on a great pedestal higher than yourself and lord over their every word? In fact the very act of trying to impress someone creates the opposite effect. Take back your decision making crown. Don't always be seeking the approval of others to justify your decisions. Don't tell the world what you are going to do, show it. We may have habitually given the responsibility of our decisions to someone else because we felt that we were not capable. We may have been told that we were stupid or laughed at in the past when we attempted to make decisions that went against the grain. Often it can be well meaning but ignorant family members that put down the dreams of a person by ridicule. Understand that your opinion is as valid as anyone else's and the most important decision maker in your life is YOU. It is no harm to seek advice from those that have a good understanding about certain things or know well. But the decision to take that advice is down to you. You can decide in the very next moment that you are going to take control of the wheel and design the life you have always wanted, not the life that someone else has wanted for you. Stop blaming others or circumstances for the conditions in your life and realize that it is YOU that is responsible for all the experiences in your life.

It's All In Your Mind

Make Your Vocation Your Vacation

Do what you like and like what you do. You spend a long time in your job. Don't let it just be a source of pain. Let's do a simple math on the subject. Let's say you work in a standard 8 hour a day job. In one year that translates into 78 complete 24-hour days in the year, taking into account 5 weeks holidays. By the age of 65 five it works out to be 10 years non-stop work. Think about that for a moment. 10 years. Add the fact that by 65 you will have slept for 20 years solid. So at 65 you will have spent half your life asleep and working. It goes without saying that 10 years is a long time. That's 10 years calculated at 24-hour days. How clever is it to spend 10 full years doing something that does not make you happy? In some cases it represents a lot of pain, a prison sentence by any standards. The secret to being successful is to choose a job that fulfils you and brings more pleasure than pain. How will you choose to spend those 10 years? Make your passion your vocation. Are you one of those people that only live to see the weekend and then find that it goes too quick? Think about how much better your life would be if you enjoyed your job. Wouldn't you put a lot more effort into it? We are conditioned to think that this is the way it has to be. That's why holidays are not called everyday. Well truthfully you can define what suits you. Take the time to think about this and have the courage to go after what you really want. It's never too late. Don't let alibis creep in and become excuses not to change. 'Oh I'm too old or how can I with the mortgage.' Trust your intuition and the answers will come to you. You should associate pain with not changing because it will cost you a lot in the long-term.

It's All In Your Mind

The Power of Decisions

In every moment of your life you are making decisions and it is these
decisions that are creating your life as you know it. Decisions about what
you are doing, going to do and what you shall not do are all affecting your
outcomes. Decisions on what to think and equally important on what not to
think and do. Just think about the various decisions you have made in the
past and understand how they have impacted on your life after that. For
example your decision to go to a certain establishment may have resulted in
you meeting your life partner. As a young child I stole a milk bottle, and got
caught. Getting caught was one of the greatest things that could have
happened to me as I then associated great pain with stealing and it prevented
me from ever thinking about doing it again. Subsequently I ended up paying
back my dues by working for the milkman. As it happened he was an avid
tourist of the Untied States and started the desire in me to visit there. So I
headed off for a summer and got a job with the airlines and ended up
spending time in Hawaii and Bermuda. After coming home I got a job in
sales with the largest US Airline in the world and travelled first class all
around the world. On one particular trip to New Orleans, I was out
socialising with a work colleague. He was tired and decided to go to the
hotel and I made a decision to stay out for a bit longer in the French Quarter.
Well, I was glad that I did because I met a young beautiful lady from
Nicaragua and she has since become my life partner. I have been to
Nicaragua almost every two months since then too. The point I am trying to
make is that each of these decisions has had a huge impact on the flow of the
rest of my life. It all stems back to the night I decided that I would steal that
milk bottle and end my first and only brush with crime. Now I'm not

recommending that someone go out and steal and hope for the best, of coarse not. What I am trying to demonstrate is how important decisions are in our life and how they send our lives in new unexpected directions. They practically ordain our destiny in every moment we take them. Sometimes we take profound decisions lightly like getting married or not calling that someone back or whatever the decision may be. The decision on who to approach and whom not to approach. Sometimes we spend more time choosing a DVD rental than on our most profound decisions. Again understanding and becoming aware of this truth is what can empower you to be more conscious of the importance of your decisions. Then there is the other side of the coin, the people who find it difficult to make any decisions at all. They are in a constant state of confusion, finding it difficult to decide what to wear, where to go and then even if they want to go out at all.

Not making a decision at all is almost as bad as making a bad one. You should learn to the process of making decisions and to stick to your decisions once they are made, unless a better alternative comes up. Get into the habit of making your decisions quickly and committing to them. Learn the strategies of decision-making and strive to improve in this very important area.

Like all psychological truths, this knowledge can be used to your best advantage. *You can decide on what to focus on at any given time.* What you focus on in the NOW is what you experience in the NOW. It is vital to focus on the things that you want and to keep your mind of the things that you do not want.

It's All In Your Mind

Self-Concept.

Your self-concept is the idea that you hold about yourself and your genuine beliefs that you have adopted about your abilities and everything about you as a person. Your mind operates in such a way that it will only accept as true things that are consistent with your self-concept. It is the real image that you hold in the back of your mind of yourself. Your mind, searches for further evidence that is in line with your self-concept or self-image and tries as much as possible to reinforce the truth of this. It is the "who I am", the instinct to have a specific identity. Its practicality in society is understandable in that it allows people to be consistent and prevents someone from being a different personality every moment of the day. A thousand split personalities if you will. So that's all fine, but the thing is that through the channel of free will we can choose the type of personalities and self-concept that we hold as true to ourselves. Certain things can change the self-concept and make us think differently about ourselves and that is what we are interested in here.

"And the Oscar goes to...."

When in a social setting we are always acting in a certain way. We are more comfortable with some people and less with others, depending on how our interactions are with them and how consistent they are with our own ego and self-image. There are those that even upon the mere mention of their name or the sight of them create a reaction in us and cause us to act in a way that we ourselves may not like, but can hardly help. This very fact can be used to your advantage. You can change who you are in the role of your life. Have you ever seen someone get a promotion to another position of responsibility and how it affects their whole personality? They have a new reference or proof to work from, and whether they like it or not, they will be acting a different role. A role that they perceive to be the appropriate for the position. I'm not suggesting that you change your whole personality, only that you improve your self-concept to be closer to that of the person whom you would like to be. It could be more confident or more outgoing or simply friendlier and more understanding.

One of the ways to do this is to imagine as clearly as possible the way you would like to be and then to focus and concentrate on this image and its manifestation. Try to think of as many details as you possibly can relate to the new you. If it is more confidence in social occasions, then see yourself handling the situation exceptionally well and with utter self-confidence. Imagine the people in the scene warming to you and how you would feel when that way. Then when it is clearest in your mind, affirm that which you would like to be, such as "I am calm and confident in all social situations. I am inspired to do and say the correct things at all times". Then do something that will anchor this in your experience such as place the tip of your thumb to your four finger and say to yourself, "When I place these two fingers together I will be able to recall this sense of confidence in an instant." Repeat it three times in the morning, afternoon and before retiring to bed. It is important that you anchor your trigger at the point when you have the clearest image in your mind and are feeling it at a peak level in your imaginary experience. We shall talk a little bit more about the application of this a little later and how you can use this to overcome stress in a variety of occasions. These techniques have been used by famous people and top athletes in all kinds of disciplines to help them gain self-confidence. You too can benefit from these effective techniques.

What you have just done is imagine an event in your future history, reinforced it with an affirmation and then anchored it in your physiology for recall at a later time. When you need to reproduce this state, then you may place your fingers together and say your affirmation, and adopt the confident stance, draw in a deep breath and you will cause a positive change in your mental state.

Most of us have been using this very process against ourselves and have restricted ourselves unnecessarily with a great degree of fear when faced in a variety of scenarios that are likely to be performance related such as making a speech or simply working in a group. The internal dialogue speaks without seize and you imagine innumerable ways that you will fail and see the various outcomes and reactions of others. Many people adopt habitual postures that cause them to induce a timid state and appearance. Take control of this process, you owe it to yourself. Note how your restrictions are holding you back and resolve to overcome them. In psychology this is termed adding leverage to the desired change.

It's All In Your Mind

Inferiority Complex

Another thing that is worth a mention at this point is the inferiority complex, whereby someone may feel that they are inferior to others in some way. It is important to become aware of it and to overcome it as soon as possible. Many people who have not gone to college believe themselves to be inferior intellectually in some way. They place the college graduate on a pedestal in their mind and feel themselves unworthy and less intelligent. This of coarse is not true. Just because you have not read certain texts and been awarded a certificate to prove that you have a degree, does not mean in any way that you are less intelligent than those that do. All it means is that you did not expend the same amount of energy in that area as they have. You are every bit as capable of doing great things. This again comes back to the suggestibility of us as humans. If we got D's in our school exams we use this as evidence or as a belief reference that WE ARE a D student. When you go to take on new tasks you may humble yourself and feel incapable again referring to your thought that "I am only a D student," I'm not smart enough to do that. I recall being poor at maths in primary school, however when I went on the secondary school I was placed in the highest class in the year. We were always told how capable we were and our maths teacher was no exception. Once it was repeated to me enough times I started to believe it. I began to prove it in my experience in the class and soon I came to love maths and done higher level in my exams. So do not put labels on yourself, unless they are of your higher potential. You can be trained and learn to do most anything you desire to do. Do not let others label you either, and if you hear people label you in such a way, use the energy bubble technique and delete the message in your mind and replace it with one more empowering.

It's All In Your Mind

Maradona was told he was too small to play football, yet he went on to become one of the world's greatest. Einstein was told he was bad at maths and a poor student in school and went on to be one of the greatest minds that ever lived. The thing is, that you too are as great as all these things. You simply have to desire them strong enough and take action. Remove the false labels and take away your limitations. Believe in yourself and be all you can be. Never finish a negative sentence about yourself such as "Too….(small) (fat/thin) (stupid) or whatever.

This goes for children too. Please be very careful how you label your children. It is important to realize,

"That which you praise grows in your experience and in your life"

So instead of limiting them for fear of disappointment, prepare them to do whatever they want and to. Realize that they can be much more than they thought. Do this by praising them for their ability to do it, and it will eventually settle in to their mind as a possibility. Very often to ridicule the behaviour of a child only serves to make them want to prove you right by doing it more.

Root out inherited restrictions and attitudes that may have clung to you by virtue of the very force of the thought that conceived them. Two people may have a specific opinion about something, and the one with the strongest conviction of thought shall dominate and have their opinion accepted as the correct one. Even if they are wrong and the other is correct. Some people are quite forceful in their opinions we even have a term for them, a very opinionated person. I'm sure that you have been in situations whereby you were quite sure you were correct, but someone else convinced you to the contrary by their apparent certainty. It is a psychological principle that the more forceful or bigger a thought is, it shall dominate smaller thought just as a wave from a large rock overcomes the ripples of a smaller stone. The same could be thought of brain waves. Even in dire circumstances a more forceful will can overcome a lesser conviction. Be more aware of how this principle works in your life. Admire people, but don't hero worship. Each human's opinion is as valid as the next to himself or herself. Recall that you are the King or Queen of your own inner kingdom. By all means listen to the more learned, and assimilate what they say, but make sure that you take into account your own intuition and opinion too. Opinions are relative. You have a right to your own opinion and so do others. Respect that opinion and realize that you have the power to choose your own. Don't be blinded by the apparent reputation, title, or fame of another. In the past, the most powerful world rulers and successful scientists of the time believed that the earth was flat. In such cases even the homeless peasant in the street may have intuitively known the world was round, having gazed at the moon and the heavens. Part of what makes us vulnerable to the opinions and perceptions of others is what may be termed the, sponsoring thought. This may be thought of as an information package that arrives via one or more of the senses, that arrives at the gates of your mind. The Gatekeeper of your mind makes an immediate deduction of which part of the brain the package needs to be sent and how it should be stamped. The Gatekeeper function of the brain accesses the memory faculty and all associations relating to the incoming package, and then stamps the package according to that schema. With the package suitably labelled it is sent on down the neural pathways with the assumption that the first impression is correct and that the attached label sums up the contents of the package correctly. The Gatekeeper then shuts the gates to any other stimuli that are not consistent with this label and belief. You can build more awareness into the Gatekeeper process in your mind, and consciously reprogram the labelling process and command the Gatekeeper to not shut the gates until other relevant information has been gathered, even if it is counter to the original first impression. The assimilation of this additional information may bring to light a truer picture of what really is contained in the information package. Marketers know all about the process of the sponsoring thought and its sister, associations. Let me go a little bit further into this process if I may.

Information comes to us via the senses; sight, smell, taste, touch and hearing. In addition to this there are extra-sensory perceptions that we all have, but it is sufficient to deal with the five senses for now.

This information reaches the Gatekeeper of the brain and is perceived as mentioned above. The perception is based on all memory and associations that have been adopted heretofore. The Gatekeeper instantly labels the information package and sends it down the neural pathways that relate most closely with the stamped perception, much like water is drawn through the branch of a tree to the outer leaves. The information package then heads down these neural pathways, firing the chemical memories and associations, and then assimilates how to react to this information in the context of that schema. For example, if we see a well-dressed woman in a suit whom introduces herself as doctor, the information is sent down a certain path in the neural highways of the brain, stimulating the associated memories and perceptions of doctor, and the image received. Thus we may assume, doctor – successful – studied a long time – intelligent – wealthy and so on, depending on your experience and associations to date relating to doctors, or woman or woman doctors. This will then cause you to view them and all they say and do through the tinted lenses of the neural links associated with the above and react accordingly. Why do you think advertisers use Doctors to endorse their products? On the other hand you may have painful memories associated with the word or image of Doctors. Perhaps you received an injection as a child from a doctor or dentist and associated great pain to even the sound of the word doctor or dentist.

The follow on is what I would call perceptual transference or what marketers call the halo effect. The halo effect is when a company with a brand known for quality and value, brings out a new product. It may even be unrelated, but consumers will perceive the product to be of quality and value based on their perceptions of the brand. So if we believe that a person such as a doctor has performed certain tasks competently in their chosen field, that they know as much about everything else. The fact is that they may know less than you in non-medical fields. I know of a judge that does not know how to change a plug, yet makes decisions that change people's lives everyday. He has absolute competence in his field, but I wouldn't ask him to rewire my house. Once again, don't let the rock of your pre-conceived ideas overcome the ripples of truth that resonate within you. Drop the inferiority complex and trust in yourself more. The Gatekeeper principle also operates in line with our self-concept and chosen beliefs. Many possibilities and opportunities may pass your way, only to be tagged by the Gatekeeper and shipped off to the self-doubt part of the brain to pick up its favourite alibis of failure along the way. It could be stamped, "Not possible, I'm too stupid, too scared…." It then stimulates the part of the brain that resonate with this failure belief. It accesses past memories of failure that validate this belief and satisfy you that you have tagged it correctly. Just as nature abhors a vacuum, the brain abhors uncertainty. It tries to label and make sense of everything and make it fit all current beliefs held in the mind. Thus tries to make sense of the blobs on a Roshark ink blot test or fashion the clouds into a familiar pattern. It likes to store information packages in the right cells and get on to something else. A bit like parking a car in a memory space. When uncertainty reigns, the cars continue to flow around the system causing traffic jams and gridlock, which can manifest in a headache or migraine. The mind dislikes uncertainty by design, and fears that which we don't understand. One of the benefits of this labelling process and Gatekeeper function is to help us filter information that we need and to ignore what we don't. Everyday we perceive billions of pieces of information. The Gatekeeper function of the brain assists us to filter out information based on our self-concept, and goals. The tools that will help us to use the Gatekeeper process shall be dealt with in the remaining chapters, such as goal setting, affirmations and visualization, and the Mind Studio system.

We are all one and everyone is equal in the imagination of God. As a part of God, you may see things the same way. You are neither inferior to others and they are not inferior to you. Learn to see the divine in everyone and everything.

It's All In Your Mind

The Kabbala Principle of Equanimity.

I came across a wonderful concept in Kabbala literature, which relates to the Kabbalistic concept of equanimity. It basically is an approach whereby you will give your all to a task but will not be slave or overly concerned about what others think of you. It is all about being indifferent to the mockery or admiration of others, while concentrating on the things that you want. There is great wisdom in this concept and it holds a key to self-confidence if really embraced. It is not to say that you shouldn't care about people or their reactions, but rather that you are not effected in the slightest by what people may think of you.

Abraham Lincoln once said "You cannot be offended without your consent." This means that it is not the words that upset you or the actions. It is your interpretation of them and how you allow them to impact you. Remember there is real power in decision and you have the power to decide how to react in all situations.

It's All In Your Mind

The Trip Switch Technique for Changing Negative Self Talk into Positive Living.

A powerful technique for helping you to gain control of your perspectives and your frame of reference is to use your knowledge of the principles of mind to bring about a happier state within yourself. Thoughts like electricity can be a powerful agent to create or destroy, depending on how they are used. What we are now going to look at is a way of literally setting up a trip switch in your brain that is triggered by a negative thought, to switch you automatically to a pre-ordained positive thought. At first it will require a good deal of discipline and effort, however when the idea is successfully passed over to the working of your subconscious mind then the process will become automatic. Here goes,

Step One:
Choose the positive statement and image that you would like your mind to default to when the switch is tripped. You may for example choose an image of your ideal scene in the future and affirm to yourself, "Every day in everyway I am getting healthier, wealthier and happier. The Universe lovingly takes care of me now and forever more and I thank God for the abundance in my life." Now you may choose your own example. Keep it relatively short, as you may find that negative thoughts can surface regularly and a short positive affirmation helps to redirect your thoughts in a more empowering direction.

It's All In Your Mind

Step Two:

As soon as you become consciously aware of a negative thought rising in your mind, imagine a little trip switch going off from the negative position to the positive position. You may choose to imagine this taking place in your mind studio (See later section), if you like, with the resulting positive image forming on your Studio Screen, along with the affirmation. So if you become aware of something like, "I can't do this speech" or "I look awful today, " imagine the sound of the switch lashing over to the positive position and affirm quickly your positive words. You may find it even more effective simply to choose a positive word, and default to it as per above. Psychologists now understand that words actually affect the chemistry in our brain and branch off and attract to them similar thoughts as we discussed earlier. You could choose a word or short sequence of words such as, health, happiness, success, love, or joy. Now don't let the simplicity of this task throw you off, it is actually a very powerful technique for gaining control of your emotions. Approach it with the idea of a game at first. Get joy from it, see it as a challenge and it is important not to view it as a mundane obligatory task, as your brain will associate habitual pain and avoid cooperating. As a child I used to play a card game called snap. In this game two people would split the deck and place cards alternatively on the table, and as soon as a similar card would drop on its like, such as a pair of Kings, the quickest would call "Snap!" and clap their hands over the table. It's a fun game for children, and I treat the positive emotion trigger in the same way, kind of like a game of snap. After a while you won't even have to think about it and you will be wired for positive thinking in the direction of what you want.

This shall help you to channel your roaming negative thoughts and meander them into a stream of your liking. One great area to start with is the poverty thought. Remember what we said earlier about what you focus on grows. Well the same is in relation to financial debt. You may be affirming that you are rich or getting rich, but you still harbour a sense of disbelief in your mind and even feel that gnawing lump of anxiety in your stomach. We can start to overcome this and help you to stream these thoughts into ones of abundance and riches. So what do you do when you feel yourself say in your inner voice, "That bill is huge, how will I ever be able to pay it? I just seem to be getting deeper and deeper in debt." Remember, that's right, "Click" the switch is thrown and followed by "Riches are flowing abundantly into my life in the correct sequence of time action and events." Or word sequence, "Abundance, wealth, success, riches." Say them out loud if you like. What you are actually doing here is recreating the circuitry of your brain. You are getting it to trigger new thoughts and the more you repeat this exercise the more effective and engrained it shall be. You will be making new neurological connections in your brain that wire you for the life of your choosing. At the very least you will be feeling happier and in control of your immediate thoughts and therefore your life.

The positive trip switch can be used in other areas also. Particularly in your self-image. If you watch people in any setting, you will find them taking opportunities to see how they look. Popping a glance in a mirror, in a reflection and all without even consciously thinking about it. Each time we do this, we trigger off an internal response that sets off the automatic or default switch we have been using since childhood. The unfortunate thing is that most of us have been using this against ourselves. So when even pretty looking people look at there reflection, an internal dialogue is triggered which usually is negative such as, "You look bad today," or "How ugly" and this is repeated over and over again throughout the day. Checking again and again as if we had grown a new head in the past half an hour. Let's use our knowledge of the trip switch mechanism in the mind and take it off default. So let the reflection of your image be a trigger for your new phrase or thought. Old habits die-hard and it takes a good deal of repetition to bring this process to the automatic stage. Of coarse there are those that have been brought up by encouraging parents or environment and are quite confident and are doing this automatically. That is the difference between the person that craves the limelight and the one that panics with even the thought of it. Much of the internal trigger words are recorded and adopted when we were younger. Insensitive comments and others stick to this old tape like a magnet. It's time to record over them and be happier within yourself.

It's All In Your Mind

Recreate Your Own Empowering Memories.

A large factor in the confidence of peak performers in an any area, is the fact that they have built up a number of reference memories in the past that demonstrate to them that they can handle the new task. These are trigger memories and they determine our level of self-confidence when we approach new challenges. The mind fears what it does not know or cannot understand, therefore it will search for any number of memories stored in your experience to date that will back up a major premise that you will be able to handle the new situation well or not. In professional circles this is the level of self-confidence that comes with experience. For example an experienced customer service manager may feel a good degree of confidence in dealing with difficult customers, no matter how irate they become. The reason is that inside the mind of this individual, the memory bank is accessed to determine if this type of situation has been dealt with before. When a flood of memories and references to similar situations that were handled in the past come to the fore of the mind, the manager remains quite calm and handles the situation in a way that he or she has found to be successful in the past. This of coarse is the confidence that comes with experience and learning. A novice on the other hand tends to be far more nervous and uncomfortable due to a lack of these references.

The powerful subconscious mind does not differentiate between a real memory and an imagined one. In fact if a thought is repeated enough with conviction it will accept such a thought as reality. This may be used to tremendous benefit to us, if we realize that we can create our own empowering memories to support us in taking on new tasks.

It's All In Your Mind

Method.

When faced with a certain challenge in the future we can visualise ourselves performing at a peak level and imagine a successful outcome, and thereby increase the likelihood of this manifesting in our experience. Energy follows thought. We can also look to, or more accurately, create a past memory by imagining clearly that you have done the task successfully a number of times before. *Affirm* that you have, *Visualise* that you have and repeat the process until you have instilled the sense of belief in your mind. In the example of public speaking, imagine as clearly as possible that you had spoken comfortably to large audiences in the past. Hear yourself speak, see the smiling faces in the crowd and the delight you felt as the words flowed through you and how successful you were. You may add the affirmation, "I will successfully _____, because I know that I have done this successfully many times in the past and am therefore uniquely qualified to do so. " Then run a number of short mental movies of you having done so in the past. Add as much feeling and excitement to the process as you can muster. If you repeat this process with feeling often enough, you will effectively impregnate your subconscious mind with your own manufactured memories. It will eventually result in you convincing yourself that you have been successful in this area in the past. Your subconscious mind will eventually take these imagined memories to be true. Couple this with imagining yourself conducting the new task with ease and you will induce a state consistent with self-confidence and a positive outcome.

It's All In Your Mind

Pain and Pleasure Principle.

At a very basic level we are guided by two sensory feedback mechanisms that influence almost all we do. They are pain and pleasure. To a great degree our decisions are based on our perceptions of how much pain or pleasure we associate to a given task or idea. Our fundamental drives are to seek pleasure and avoid pain. We have associated both these sensations with all things throughout our lives. In a way they help us to learn and progress. For example we associate pain to touching something hot and pleasure to eating something nice. It is nature's program of sensory feedback and stimulus response to ensure that we learn and remember to do things in a certain way. The issue comes when like all of our greatest gifts we can often abuse the principle and become lazy or apathetic to taking action. A lazy person may associate more pain to going out and working than sitting on a couch and veging out seven days a week. On the other hand, a hard working person associates more pain to being out of work as it impacts on his or her self-image as a financially independent person, and it would be more emotionally painful for them and against their self-concept to be out of work. They would not be able to retain that sense of identity. This is were we can use this principle to our advantage by associating pleasure to the things we would like to do and to associate pain to not doing it. This does take mental effort, so your desire to succeed must be sufficient as to set you on your way. Take some time to think about your self-concept. What is your self-identity and what way does Pain and Pleasure influence you? The concept of pain and pleasure influences most of, if not all, of our actions and even takes precedent over the logical reasoning part of the mind. The coarse of action and decisions we make are based on how much we apportion pain

42

or pleasure to the act in question. For example a person may well know that alcohol won't do them any good in excessive quantities, and may be fully aware of the consequences of over doing it, but the pleasure associated with the immediate gain is what causes him or her to grab the coat and head for the pub or the nightclub to guzzle the night away. As a child, I had witnessed first hand the effects of alcohol on people that I cared about and as a result associated a huge amount of pain to the act of drinking and have never touched a drop in my life. When someone awakes on a cold morning for work or college, they may remain underneath the warm covers for as long as they possibly can because they link more pleasure to staying there than getting out of the bed in the cold air. It is only at the point when they associate more pain with being late and the ensuing rush that they arise from the bed and take to their heels. That in short is the mechanism that drives most of our actions. Be aware of it and understand its role in shaping so much of your actions or as is often the case the lack of action.

The way to use this knowledge to your benefit is to construct links between the things that you don't want with pain, and the things you would like to do with pleasure. In the example of the person who would like to give up drinking alcohol or at least reduce the tendency to drink to excess, they should learn to produce neurological links with the act and the pain that it ultimately causes. So in the height of the pain sensations it is important to apportion the link to the root cause. Assimilate the link in your mind, affirm it, "It is the alcohol that caused this, and I banish alcohol from my life." It is more important to appeal to your emotions than it does to your logic if you are to create change and the actions needed to produce it. Most behaviour change therapies work along these principles, especially the eradication of bad habits such as smoking. In the example of smoking, one lists all the nasty effects of the habit such as black lungs, poor health and may even involve a visit to a cancer ward. The clearer and more striking the image holds the more it will register on our emotions. The implications of these images on the self-concept should be considered, as the more you relate these conditions to you and understand what they are cheating you out of, such as good health, then you will begin to register the implications they have on your own life. Thus you will be stacking the case against the behaviour.

Stress and Anxiety

There is no doubt that the pressures of modern living have had an impact on the emotional well-being of many people in society. The pace has quickened and some are struggling to keep up. This has been termed the information age and those that are not qualified in certain areas of discipline are left behind. Many working environments are less than healthy with poor access to sunlight, little movement and poor ventilation. Many corporations are working in a multi laired environment with mini office societies operating within each building. Often individuals on the lower rungs of the corporation are viewed as inferior to the folks in the position just above them. Sometimes the personality types that are determined to get the promotions are not always the individuals with the best people skills in the world and they end up having a negative influence on the atmosphere in an office akin to bullying. There are others who remain in abusive relationships and feel smothered and desperate for a change, but don't have the courage to take a chance. Another form of stress that people are under is the self-imposed stress. People have a desire to stand out and to be unique and different. They want to self-actualise and have an identity that is admired by others. Very often there is a great disparity between the life that they had dreamed of and the reality in which they find themselves on a daily basis. House prices may seem out of their reach, the relationship of their dreams had not materialized yet or they are doing a job, which they know is below their station. It may be comforting to note that this is not uncommon and most people feel it to a certain degree. We are a striving race. It is built into our very DNA, and is the purpose instinct that is built into us all. It is the very same drive that has driven humankind to the moon and built supersonic jetliners and climbed the highest mountains and explored the lowest depths of the oceans. So do not feel despaired with this feeling of discontent with your lot. Mother Nature has placed it there to keep us all progressing to our higher potential. This all may not be too comforting to you, as you think about the vacuum between where you are and where you want to go. Despair not because you have in your hands a guide that shall help you both to choose to be happy in the moment and to go after your dreams and achieve them on any scale that you desire.

"Aim for the moon, but if you miss do not despair for you are among the stars"

What you may be suffering from is a case of low self–esteem. Before we can effectively implement the concepts of change and improvement, you need to do two things. One is raise your self-esteem and the other is to alter your self-image to allow the change to take place. Going back to that self-talk that we mentioned earlier. This self-talk is consistent with your deep-seated self-image and level of self-esteem. Your powerful subconscious mind is always listening and producing the objects of your thoughts. In order to change the negative self-talk, we will need to do what I would call backward induction. That is let the self-talk take the message back to the inner workings of your subconscious and reprogram the mind at the deeper levels of consciousness. The same levels that work from your memory and that trigger off reactions to certain circumstances in you. We shall use these techniques to banish some of your fears and phobias. Let's deal with the self-esteem part first. It is important to deal with this aspect of your personality first in order to establish a belief that you can achieve that which you are setting out to achieve.

From the very outset of your being born you are a winner. If you think otherwise, you have allowed the opinions of others to stick to you like mud. It is time to shower away this debris and detritus that has clung to your mind for far too long. Most of it occurred through past ridicule and opinions that we accepted by you as true. You are born with one of the most powerful Bio-computers in the Universe. It is capable of doing innumerable things beyond your wildest dreams. That exceptional piece of equipment is the brain in your head. There are literally billions of cells inside it. Now no matter what level you are operating at realize that you are only doing so through a limited strategy. You are not stupid, you do not have a bad memory as you have so often told yourself or others have told you. You are simply not using your brain in the correct and most efficient way. Most of us are not. You can change this by desiring to learn the strategies and ways of using your brain in a more effective way. Choose a person whom you believe is very bright and ask yourself "what would this person do in this circumstance?" and conduct yourself in a way that mimics this. After all, you have been mimicking people around you since you were a young child, whether you are conscious of it or not. Now you can choose your own role models and act as if you are as smart and effective as they are.

Secondly, most people worry about their appearance and wonder what others will think of them in all kinds of situations. Stop for a moment and think about how that is restricting you. This is giving away your power and thought energy again. What other people think of you is none of your business. People's thoughts belong to themselves and you should not keep trying to imagine the negative things that people will be thinking about you. In reality most people, by design of the ego or the I part of their personality are spending most of the time thinking about their own life situations. If you really realized how little time others actually spend worried about your appearance, you would probably be insulted. So stop concerning yourself with thoughts and worries about what others think. The important thing is what you think, and to ensure that it is a positive outlook. It is no harm to take pride in your appearance, but it is not beneficial to beat yourself up and feel inadequate because you do not have the perfect figure as determined by the fashion magazines and newspapers. This goes back to being aware of how these images and messages are impacting on your mental well-being. Decide now to be happy the way you are or do something about it. Don't waste you energy worrying about what others think, focus on being content within yourself. Do not feel inferior to others because you believe that they are far more educated or capable than you. Take a doctor for example, of coarse they are smart and intelligent and to be respected, but you also have inside your head the capability of doing the same as he or she. You have a wonderful brain, and had you spent as many hours studying and as many years in college as he or she, it is likely that you too would be as effective a doctor. They have simply expended more time and energy in that area than you. They are certainly not better as a human being. Leonardo De Vinci remarked that people would not consider him a genius if they only knew how hard he worked to achieve the results that he got.

Now, let's examine the idea I mentioned about sending the message back to your powerful subconscious mind. Your mind is made up of the conscious mind, your subconscious mind, and your superconscious mind. What does that mean? In simple terms, your conscious mind is the level of consciousness that you use to do simple tasks such as picking up a pen and writing or reading a book. Your subconscious mind is the automatic or subjective part of your mind. It is incalculably powerful and regulates everything from your heartbeat to your lungs and breathing. It contains all the memories of your past experiences and runs all the automatic functions, the autonomic system, of your body. It is a faculty through which you may receive intuitions and indeed is the part of the brain that heals your wounds when you cut yourself or do yourself an injury.

"The doctor dresses the wound, but it is God who heals it. "

It has stored in it your self-concept and acts in accordance with your self-esteem in terms of how it animates your body and sends you ideas that are consistent with the image that you had held of it. The superconcsious mind contains all the memory of the past. It is a part of the infinite intelligence and infinite well of love, and divine creator of the universe. Religions refer to this level as God. The way to tap into this level is through the subconscious mind and with a mixture of a strong desire, affirmations, emotionalised visualisation, faith, belief and repetition.

There is a section on the methods of affirmations and creative visualization in the coming chapters. We shall deal mostly with the conscious and subconscious minds in this section.

First I want you to write down on a sheet of paper these sentences, which you should read to yourself with feeling. The very act of writing is sending a message to this level of mind that you are serious about what you are placing in writing. It is an action that demonstrates your commitment to it. Not only is the message kept as an image in your mind, but also transmuted through the electromagnetic system of nerves to your hands and translated onto paper.

Here is a suggested affirmation that should be read first thing in the morning and before going to sleep at night.

"I am a part of the divine being and one with the universe. I like myself and thank God for all the gifts and blessings that are pouring forth on me. I feel healthy, I feel happy, I feel terrific. I am confident in all I do and say and all that I am, and am to be. I am attractive and love all people and all things. I am capable to doing anything. I am calm and confident in all situations, and am divinely inspired to do and say the correct things in the correct sequence in time actions and events and the universe lovingly takes care of me now and forever. "

It's All In Your Mind

Another powerful technique is as follows. Each time you look at yourself in a mirror say to yourself and that you like yourself. I know that it may seem silly, I was one of the people that laughed at these techniques, however the more I studied the effects of these methods, the more I realized their wisdom. A piece of advice is not to try to do such an exercise in a group, because like congenial conversation among friends it cannot be manufactured falsely and may only serve to throw you off. It must be believable to you. You should promise yourself that if you do these exercises that you will do them with an open mind and commit to doing them properly and not half-heartedly. Even the most seemingly confident people can be seen checking their appearance in a reflection on a regular basis. What we want to do is every time you see your reflection in the mirror or in a reflection say in your mind a word, "attractive," or "beautiful" or "I like you"

What this does is begin to change the automatic trigger mechanism or habitual feeling response that you used to experience when you saw your reflection in the mirror and said those terrible things to yourself. The purpose is to change the automatic habit at the deeper level of mind and to change the way you think about yourself.

Concentrate only on positive thoughts about yourself for a set period and repeat with feeling your written affirmation when you think of it. A very effective technique for deep programming can be found in the chapter on relaxation techniques.

It's All In Your Mind

Let us now examine a way of gaining control of your sources of stress. In the majority of cases the reason people are overwhelmed by fear in doing a task is that they envision it as being far bigger and intense than it actually is. In their mind they exaggerate the pitfalls and imagine things going horribly wrong and feel themselves inadequate to carry out the task. In sport the boxer may think the champion unbeatable and his mind brings that reality into how he interacts with that person. They are overwhelmed by the sponsoring thought that the other is "greater than thou"

Another reason people become stressed is due to what I would term *mental stacking*. They try to handle a myriad of tasks in their mind and progressively feel less capable to handle that which they have to deal with. An example would be the executive with a mounting pile of paperwork. While he is trying to handle the current task, his mind wanders to the large pile on the desk and begins to imagine how he would handle these tasks. Then becomes concerned that the amount is too much and if he cannot finish the work, begins to worry about how the boss or supervisor may react. Thus the concentration on the task at hand has waned and the mind is filled with a stack of scenarios, of which it is not given the time or resources to deal with sufficiently added to which it is busy directing the argument with the supervisor. In some cases the imagination quickly goes on to imagine what would happen if he lost his job, and then creates a scene that will take place with the wife at home. All the while the stress hormones and adrenal gland are working over time and the body is reacting as if the threatening images were real. The exec. then becomes more stressed and his memory becomes affected as blood and oxygen are directed to other parts of the brain instead. As this keeps up the powerful subconscious provides some pet warnings in the body, shots across the bow if you will. A mild panic attack here, a racing heart beat there and lethargy, until if ignored long enough decides to shut the system down by saying, "Enough is enough, I tried to warn you but you didn't listen and now I have to shut down the operation until you avoid this behaviour in the future," It is natures way of protecting the person from further harm and it is vital to listen to your body as it gives you these little warnings. They are warning indicators that are trying to tell you about the affect that these behaviours are having on your internal system and your body.

The way to deal with mental stacking is to simplify your tasks in your mind. Learn to prioritise by order of importance and resolve to do one thing at a time.

You only have two hands and two feet and are not disposed to handle all the tasks that you place in your mind as per the above example. The best way to gain a sense of control is to realize that you are to handle and concentrate on *ONE task at a time.* When you feel your mind wandering off to tasks that you haven't got around to yet, mentally say to yourself. "One task at a time" Do not try to juggle too much at the same time or you will drop the lot. The above is just as relevant in the home, where you may keep putting off a bunch of tasks and place them in mental notes. They are always there as to do's. Try not to do this. This form of procrastination is the same as mental stacking and hinders your performance, as these things will be sitting there in the back of your mind.

It's All In Your Mind

Make a list of things and place them in order of importance and work your way down from the most important first and so on. It is best to work it out on paper as the very act of writing it forms a feedback evidence to your mind that you are taking some action towards the purpose that it has set forth. Clear the haze. A lot of tasks mounting in your mind create a sense of confusion, a muddled head and a kind of cloud over you. Take action. Once you get into the habit of taking action you will find that you will begin to build momentum. So that to do list will turn into a have done list, and is usually followed by a sense of satisfaction at having accomplished something. Give yourself a reward after completing the list. Add some pleasure leverage to your mind and reward yourself with some treat. This will help to reinforce the behaviour and increase the chance of it becoming a new habit.

There is a useful phrase that helps when one is in a stressful situation that represents some kind of painful experience, and that its to realize that things are always in a state of change. Even the Universe itself is in a constant state of flux. Once accompanied with the breathing exercises in this book the following phrase helps to change the minds perspective of a situation. When one is feeling the onset of panic, one should take in a deep breathe through the nose and hold it for a couple of seconds and release it through the mouth and say to yourself,

"This too shall pass"

A factor in panic is that you may feel that the pain of the situation, or the situation itself may last forever. In truth it shall be gone with the passing of time, like other experiences. In order to help yourself along after saying this a couple of times you should cast your mind forward to a pleasant experience to which you are looking forward to and imagine being there now. Add as much detail as you can and affirm your control. Then you may use one of the previous confidence triggers that I discussed earlier.

Sponsoring Image and Trigger Words Technique.

The following is an effective technique for calling up certain resourceful states at will. The famous conditioning research done by Pavlov, has a good deal of relevance in how we can begin to condition ourselves to behave in ways that we would like. In short, Pavlov had set up experiments whereby he had a group of dogs in a set environment. Every time he would feed the animals he would ring a bell prior to providing the food. The dogs soon began to associate the bell with food and any time he rang the bell, the dogs would salivate knowing food was on the way. Even after numerous experiments of ringing the bell and the absence of food, the dogs continued to salivate. They had a conditioned response to the bell. As we grow up, we too are conditioned in many ways to respond to signals in our environment. We are now going to use this knowledge to start conditioning ourselves for to gain control of our emotions and to feel the way we would like to feel on a more consistent basis. We are going to learn to ring our own bell.

A second piece of information that is important to us here is what I call the sponsoring image. Our minds are designed to filter out incoming messages in a way that allows us to concentrate on specific tasks or ideas at a time. This for the most part is useful, however it does mean that we filter out some useful information too. In short we simply don't notice certain information that reaches us through our various senses. For example, when you first see a well dressed man in an expensive suit you assume that the person is well to do, and is in a responsible position. You do not know these things, but you in fact assume them based on the associations you have linked in the past when you saw such a well-dressed person. We make these assumptions all the time, and our brain is designed to search what it knows and to link neurologically a set of believes regarding a thing. Once the information has been linked to your set of beliefs, the seeking function of the brain switches off and is happy that you have identified incoming information accurately. You will even continue to rationalise your initial impression even though other conflicting information may come to light, in fact your mind will begin to scramble to justify your initial impression and seek to validate it. A great example of this can be found in the life of Frank Abagnale Jr. of whom the movie "Catch Me If You Can" was based. He was able to cash fraudulent checks all across America by wearing a Pilot's uniform, and the mere sight of the pilot uniform made the bank clerks assume that he was legitimate, even though he was a confidence man. So with your understanding of this principle and how our brains operate we can now look at how to use this knowledge to control our own emotions.

First let's begin by setting up our own sponsoring image. The idea is to choose and concentrate upon a specific image in order to open the door to a conditioned desirable state. As in affirmations, it is important that the image has a specific set of feelings attached to it. The ideal feeling we are looking for is *joyous expectancy.* Note that the language of your soul often speaks to you through your feelings. Pay attention to what happens in your body. If you find it difficult to imagine an inspiring image then you can use an image or picture that you can focus your attention on. You may even use a success collage of your ideal scene. The important thing is that you feel a jet of excitement when you concentrate on the image. Know that is true and is possible for you. If the image you use is an imagined one, concentrate on it in as much details as possible. Play with your imagination, feel yourself actually in the image and experience the sights, sounds, smells and sensations attached to it. Work on making it clear and bright in your mind. Once you are feeling the desirable sense of excited expectancy. You may reinforce the effect by playing a song that helps capture such feelings too. For practical purposes you should now choose a trigger word that you attach to this image and feeling. It may be any word of your choosing and should be repeated to yourself over and over again while the image and sensations are present. What you are actually doing is setting up a link, a ringing bell, by attaching the specific magic word to the feeling you have. Repeat the process as often as is practical. By doing so you shall set up a neurological trail to this feeling, and can use it when you need by simply uttering the word to yourself in your mind. This shall act as a key to the door of your most joyous moods. A holistic way to get the coffee high without the caffeine! You may use several trigger words to which your mind shall associate a branch of neurological links and sensations. It could be your own magic word, one that you make up. You may even use Abracadabra if you like. The effect is truly magical, and if repeated enough and linked effectively, will allow you to call upon this mood by simply creatively using the stimulus of your word to create the response in your mind.

The Power Walk

Another very simple but effective technique I sometimes use is what I call the *Power Walk.* The power walk is simply making a mental statement with each step and stride you take. Raise your chin, hold your shoulders high, stride with confidence, draw in deep breaths through the nose and out the mouth, and mentally say words that will empower you. With the impact of each step say love, health, wealth, happiness, confidence, courage..etc. Each word should be imagined as the impact and vibrations of your step run through your body. Repeat often and soon the very act of walking shall trigger the words like a mantra in your mind and attract the qualities and like thoughts in your mind that you desire. These thoughts and your upright walk will begin to manifest a new confidence in you and crowd out any negative thoughts that may have arisen in the past.

It's All In Your Mind

Creating Your Own Inner Sanctuary to Overcome Panic and Fear.

A very simple yet effective technique for helping you to remain calm in a circumstance or environment that would normally cause you panic is to create a place in your imagination where you may retreat to at will. It could be a rock pool in a cave, a room in your house, a nice pleasant place you visited once, the inside of a glass bubble, any place that you would consider a relaxing, calm and pleasant place to be would suffice. So when you are in a calm mood visit the place in your mind. Imagine the sights, sounds, smells, feelings, even the taste of the air. In a relaxed state remain there and take a look around you, affirm to yourself,

"At the centre of my being is a calm, relaxed, safe place where I am now" Repeat this exercise a number of times and then when you find yourself in a stressful environment, take a deep breath and in your mind go to your safe haven, and affirm the above. You will find that it will help you gain a greater degree of control in circumstances that would otherwise have thrown you into a panic. The more often you visit your safe haven in a relaxed state, the more effective it will be when you need to feel that state in a stressful situation.

It's All In Your Mind

Habits...The Tracks of Rabbits!

We are more predictable than you think. Everyday we are subject to the electromagnetic tracks in our mind. Like the rabbit that uses the same track everyday our habits are based on a kind of survival mechanism built into our brains. It works on the logic that this behaviour worked before and you survived and are safe so you may do it again safely. The process can be like the needle going around in the groves of a record. The more emotional intensity we have with an activity the more deep the groove and the clearer the track. Habits can be good or bad and usually require the repetition of the behaviour over a number of days, usually about ten to twelve before it is established as a persistent habit. They become deeply ingrained electrical patterns in the brain and can sometimes last a lifetime if no conscious effort is made to change them. Like the other principles, habits can work for or against you depending on the kind of habits you form. Some habits go on to form into OCD's (Obsessive Compulsive Disorders). These are odd habits that people form, which as the name suggests, compels the individual to behave in a certain way on a daily basis. It is very common in society and many people with the disorder are not even aware of it. This behavioural aberration may manifest in the form of plucking hairs, chewing nails, peeling skin from the lips, or checking that the gas is off or the door locked many times. Others will leave the phone to ring a certain amount of times, and have a neurological link that makes them feel that something bad will happen if they do not conduct this ritual. These are habits taking on a more extreme form. They are generally caused by an emotional upset at some time in the past and when seeking comfort had established the behaviour as a distraction. It becomes so firmly established that the person may not be able to stop it, and in some cases girls pull their entire hair out one hair at a time.

You may replace bad habits with good ones for a more empowering daily routine. I recommend substituting a bad habit with one that is good for you. Instead of going for a pint of alcohol, go for a walk. Instead of eating chocolate eat fruit. It is important that the new habit offers a similar pleasure or benefit, or you could lapse back into the old habits with the passing of time.

With habits such as the hair plucking, it may be difficult to change, as they are often not aware of it. It helps to actually consciously do the habit and think about it as you are doing it. Rather than force yourself to try to give it up. This has proved successful with habits such as nail biting and it was found that when an individual went to bite the nails at a time when they didn't automatically feel like it, and observed the sensation while consciously doing it they felt it to be undesirable and often the habit would soon disappear.

We are habitual creatures and tend to establish daily routines with remarkable similarity. For example one may get the bus at the same time each morning and sit on the same side of the bus everyday and walk the same path everyday and so on. Even the choice of shop or airline that you fly may be habitual. This is part of our comfort zone and there is not much wrong with it except that it stifles change and does not compel an individual to try new things as often as they could.

It's All In Your Mind

Believe it or not, even being late can become a habit. The way to form a beneficial habit is to repeat a behaviour several times a day and continue to do so for about three weeks and by that time the neurological pathways in the brain will be firmly established and learned. Practice is the same as habit forming, with the added dimension that you are consciously checking for feedback and improving yourself accordingly.

The Importance of Imagination!

Einstein stated, " Imagination is more important than knowledge." There is a great deal of validity in that statement. It was the imagination that has created the wonderful airliners, ocean liners, rockets, medicines and massive cities. It was the power of imagination that created the fantastic works of Leonardo De Vinci, the plays of Shakespeare and the fabulous movie industry. All of these things come from the imagination. Even our very cultures and the reality that we live everyday were dreamed up in the imaginations of our forefathers. The degree to which we use our imaginations determines the limits we place on our very lives. Take for example this very day. There are infinite things that you could have done today, or could do today, tomorrow this year, but only by our failing to use our imagination we limit the very scope of our experiences. You could decide to write a book, climb the Himalayas for charity, start a business, and visit an old relative that you haven't seen in years. May I take a quick moment to advise you to get rid of one of the most detrimental enemies of success and that's the negative alibis. "I don't have enough time, " Sure how could I afford that." That's nice, Noel, but reality is different." Take stock of these for what they really are. They are detrimental to you achieving greater success in your life. We even have our favourite alibis, the ones that we use regularly and with a kind of endearing affection and twisted pride. "Sure I don't have the brains for that" "I'm too slow, stupid, " I don't have a note in my head" Then after making the statement we are happy to let them be the end all and be all of that situation and stop us every time. One of the most common ones is "I don't have enough time." If you desire something strong enough and genuinely want to achieve a result you will succeed. If you wanted to write a book, you would go to bed one hour earlier and get up at 6am before work and write your heart out. *Remember there is power in awareness.* At least if you understand what these false alibis are cheating you out of and how they hinder you from even trying a task, then you will at least be deciding your faith instead of letting your alibis switch you off by default.

Getting back to the imagination. It is the key to all progress and creation. There are infinite resources and infinite possibilities around us and within us all the time. We are always simply one idea away from being a millionaire and helping our fellow humans and other inhabitants of this planet. Ideas are the offspring of the imagination and all abundance and prosperity begin with an idea. Take the Eiffel Tower for example, that had to originate in the imagination of someone in the form of an idea. The idea is like the seed and when it reaches a fertile mind it begins to grow until it manifests in the material plane for all to see. Give me one man with a vision and a fertile imagination and he can conquer the world. First comes the idea, then the application of the imagination and then the planning and the physical action and the manifestation. Begin to take note of the creative forces that exist all around us and that operate within and through us. Realize that with the power of your imagination you can create the life of your dreams and contribute greatly to humanity. At the very least you will improve your experience of life. So as you become aware of this force, observe it operate all around you. The next time you watch a movie, think upon the ideas and the imaginative processes that were used in order to bring this film into being. Think upon the creative minds that made the TV on which you watch it. Understand that the very light that illuminates your room was conceived in the imagination of a person just like you. The great Thomas Edison had imagined it first as an idea and then used his imagination to create it. It is the way God works through us, and the more we use our imaginations the closer we get to the God in us. We are like siphons at an infinite lake. The more you use your imagination the more you draw from the great source and the flow of ideas shall increase exponentially. Especially if your ideas are for the betterment of the planet and mankind, and you will tap the very source of infinite ideas. It's worth reminding you that *all that you could ever want in this life are available to you through the faculty of your imagination.* One idea can be enough. But like the seed of a great sequoia tree, it must fall on a receptive mind otherwise it shall remain just that, a seed of infinite potential that remains untapped. In order for an idea seed to grow it must be nourished with imagination and persistent action towards its realization.

It's All In Your Mind

Improve Your Senses and Get More Out Of Life.

You can improve your senses beyond what you may have thought possible. Up until now the likelihood is that you have only been barely using the five senses let alone incorporating the sixth sense. The elite forces of the military learn to use their senses; even hunters have by the nature of their job learned to enhance their senses more effectively. In the urban jungle however the brains natural defence has been to desensitise a lot of the noise pollution around us. This has resulted in the lowering of our sensory experiences. The sense of smell can differ widely between people and some have such acute senses that they can smell the scent of someone that may have been in the room five hours before, not withstanding that the person had normal hygiene standards of coarse. The way to improve your senses is to use them more in a focused way. When passing flowers stop and smell their wonderful scent. Start to use your senses a lot more. Listen more closely to sounds that you had previously filtered out. The subconscious has a natural filter that tends to only allow the senses to bring to you that which is part of your self-concept and your major goals or purpose. Also if like many others you have been using self-talk against yourself, you need to change the way you speak of your senses. We all know of the disappearing salt and pepper problem. You're asked to get the salt from the kitchen and you enter the kitchen with something else on your mind, or worse you throw you shrug your shoulders and say out loud, "I can't see the salt. I can't find it anywhere…it's not here." Then someone else follows you in and plucks it off the table in front of you. It was right there in front of your eyes as plain as day, yet you couldn't see it. This is due to the process of self-talk and self-programming. Your brain followed the thought pattern and listened to the commands of your affirmations that "can't see .." and hence you could not see it.

So change the way you talk about your ability, because your subconscious is always listening to that inner voice and taking the content as commands to bring into your reality.

We see with our brain and not our eyes alone. In cases were people have recovered their sight after many years, and particularly those that were born blind, have a very difficult time understanding the images and colours that suddenly flash into their mind. Even though the eye function had been restored the brain had to learn to decipher shapes again. For the first few weeks the world would appear as a hazy, pastel wash of colours and shapes that they could not make sense of them. They would have to go through a lengthy learning process of teaching the brain that the shape of an apple was an apple and often they would have to feel the object before they would recognise it. We have done this as children. It is the healthy curiosity and exploration that we see taking place as the infant fumbles about and examines everything. The child see its, touches it and as we know all too well even tries to taste and eat it.

Start paying attention to the multitude of sensory feedback that is around you and you will awake from the kind of sleep walking existence that may have trapped you in a bubble before you became aware of it. It can be a bit like when on an airplane you feel fine, you hear things fine. Then you pop your ears after a while and the volume and clarity doubles in an instant.

It's All In Your Mind

That's only a physiological adjustment, but the adjustments you make in your mind shall be even more profound.

Your subconscious mind responds to purpose. You should make it a habit to always specify to your brain the exact purpose of any activity you do. A lot of the time we do this inferentially and without much thought. Your brain functions much more efficiently when given a clear purpose and an indication of exactly what you want from it.

The next time you are walking in the park, pay attention to the noises about you. The sounds of the birds singing in the distant woods, the sound your feet make when walking. The sound of your breathing and feel out your heart beat without placing your hand over it. Pay attention to the temperature of your body and how the air feels against your skin. How does the air smell?

If you are in a street pay attention to the sounds of the car's wheels, to the hum of the multitude of conversations going on around you. There are thousands of sounds that we choose to tune out for practical purposes on a daily basis. This exercise is wonderful in helping you understand that we are in a kind of sleep walking existence and it is time to wake up to life and your potential.

You can do this with all kinds of activities. While listening to a live CD, visualize the artist on stage and the screaming crowd the wonderful atmosphere and close your eyes imagining that you are among the crowd.

It's All In Your Mind

Imagine the stage set up and actually feel that you are there. It is amazing how this simple technique can enhance your experience of listening. It brings the other senses into the experience. You may experience a meal at a whole new level of enjoyment. The body's ability to transmute food into energy is a magical process and one that should be celebrated. When you eat an orange for example, engage the senses and pay attention to each burst of juice. Think upon the energy that it is transferring to you. Imagine the bright sunshine, and the rich soil it grew in bringing you all the goodness and energy that you need. Think of where it came from. This may also help you to stop eating foods that are not too good to you as you realize what you may be placing in your body.

The bottom line is that you can increase your basic awareness of life by engaging the senses in a more conscious way.

A Change in Perception.

Some simple changes in your perception can change the way you view your life. Did you know that, you own swimming pools, snooker halls, million dollar bars, cinemas and parklands? It's all yours as a free citizen. Think about it for a moment. For less than very reasonable charges you can visit a pool that is maintained and heated for you and staffed all year. That's right, if you live in a normal free economy these are your rights. The only difference between you and a tremendously wealthy person who actually owns one is that you just need to adjust your schedule so that it fits with public sessions. In many ways you don't have to worry about the heating and cleaning bills. The modern town or city has a wealth of facilities that you can utilise with a simple bus journey. The problem is that when things are free or cost us little we place less value on them. Take libraries for example, a wealth of information, yet taken for granted to an astounding degree. An exercise for you now is to complete the following statement,

"I am extremely wealthy as a free citizen because…"

Take the time to actually think about it. If you find that your environment does not support you being in a happy state, you can take action and place yourself in a more pleasant area. When writing my current book, I would go to the ocean on nice days and write in the serenity that exists there. However, when the weather is not so good I go to the most luxurious hotels and for the price of a coffee have myself a multi million-dollar office, complete with customer service. It's simply a change in perception.

Go to museums and parks. You have more resources than you think, and just because you don't have it in your back yard and can stop others from entering, doesn't mean that you receive the same benefit. Its more fun to share experiences with others anyway. See your city or even your country as your house and it's gardens. I recommend this and when you realize that, you will feel the sense of abundance. I call this clever prosperity. It is a simple way to start to feel the abundance NOW and once you begin to get a sense of abundance your mind will be a better repository for ideas that shall help bring you personal wealth and happiness.

It's All In Your Mind

The Power of Love and Passion.

"The plan of divine love is to draw back to itself that which it loves; it draws everyone out of themselves and out of all created reality, totally into the unrelated."
Angela of Foligno

Love everything in your life. Realize that everything is energy and one of the most powerful forms of energy is love. We are in a relationship with the Oneness of the universe and our thoughts are causal in our interactions with both people and things. Our thoughts about things, people, institutions, countries, determine our perception and our relationship with them. Never hold malice in your heart against anyone, or anything. You get back what you send out. Send out love and when asked what you think about something say, "I love it". You may know someone that says they hate a certain country or its people, and when they go there or deal with them, they send out that energy and their experience confirms their animosity. The subconscious mind takes the statement as true and sends off the very signals and energy that results in bad experiences in that country. The same goes for business, department stores, and post offices, anywhere you have to deal with others. You may find that you have a certain dislike for a particular store or business and find that you seem to be invisible when you are there and that the staff treats you with indifference. Here's a little challenge for you. The next time you anticipate going to such a place or doing business there, imagine clearly how you would like it to be. Affirm it in your mind, and mentally project love and happiness to the people whom you shall be dealing with. Say in your mind, as if talking to them directly, "I send you love and happiness." Imagine that they can pick up on this thought. See what happens. You may find the difference in your interactions quite remarkable. Then when you deal with them, mentally repeat that you send them love and happiness. The very statement results in subtle changes in behaviour that are picked up by those whom the thoughts are directed and creates the experience. Love is the highest emotion we can have. It banishes fear and drives away the shadows and the darkness. The Beatles made the point well when they said, "All you need is love, love is all you need!" It's so true. Get into the habit of telling yourself that you love everyone and everything in your life. You will be amazed at how this shall change the way you interact with the world around you. Because primarily it changes you, and when you change you, your world effectively changes too. The Bible says love thy enemies. There is infinite wisdom in this statement. By loving something you banish the negative effects it may have had on you. Make an earnest commitment to love all things in your life. It must be an unconditional love, and once you get into the habit of demonstrating love, you will see the changes in your life and in the lives of those around you. The next time you are asked about a country you are about to visit, say "I love that country and am looking forward to going there".

It is in our nature to love and to seek love. So make sure that your job is a labour of love. Make it something that you enjoy and be one of those people that say, "I love my job" Even if you currently don't, try an experiment beginning now. When you awake in the morning say to yourself, "I love my job. I love working for ____. I send _____ love and happiness." Say it to yourself during the day also. Continue to do so for a number of days and note the results. You will find that slowly but surely your work circumstances will begin to change. One of the reasons is that you will be projecting signals, body language, and waves of thought energy of love radiating from you. You shall effectively change your personal atmosphere and anyone that comes into contact with you will recognise the positive change. If your circumstances do not change over time, then you should listen to your intuition as it may be guiding you to a different calling that is more favourable to your goal in life. Show love, *project* it and you will receive it too. Like thoughts attract like thoughts. It is one of the most important shifts you can make in your mindset. For some it will represent a real challenge and a huge change in attitude and behaviour. So the next time someone, takes your parking spot, that's right send them love and blessing. Speak the blessing and wish them well. This does not mean that you are to allow yourself to be walked all over, far from it. What it means is that you will begin to experience far more love in your life than you thought possible. Once you do that, you will never want to go back.

Appreciation.

Be thankful for everything that comes your way. There is a hidden power in appreciation. For when you praise, bless and are thankful for certain things in your life, you magnetise yourself to that very thing. Thus attracting more of it to you. Your subconscious mind acknowledges the appreciation signal as a command to increase more of the same. So when you are fortunate enough to receive a blessing thank God for it and show your appreciation. In order to demonstrate your true appreciation you will need to step up your emotional intensity and be happy and excited when expressing your appreciation. Your face and whole body should be joyous and happy. The more *feeling* you add to your words the more powerful and effective they become. I repeat that it is the level of feeling that you add that will determine the effectiveness of your thankful prayers. When you give someone a gift, you like to see the joy on their expression do you not? If you have a nice date with a wonderful person, thank God for it and send him or her thoughts of love. If you are in a relationship, affirm your love for the other person often in your mind. Go even one step further by sending them your thoughts of love, say their name and tell them you love them as if they were standing right in front of you. The thought vibration will reach them no matter where they are.

Even plants respond to love and attention and grow in abundance in its presence. By providing love and attention you are sharing positive energy with the object of your concentration and focus. You are like the candle giving light. So by the same logic, do not harbour any thoughts of hatred or anger or discord to anyone for it will effect you most of all. It actually affects your body. That's why aggressive people often end up with ulcers and many health problems.

Live life with a sense of passion, and enthusiasm. I saw a program on the Discovery Channel about an emergency ward in a New Orleans hospital. I was impressed at the dedication and enthusiasm of the surgeons that were interviewed, and how they went on about loving their job. They even described the long night hours as "fun" and welcomed the responsibility. Hence they performed their duty exceptionally well and loved every moment of it. These were happy and productive people who enjoy life to the full. If they enjoy their career so much I can only imagine how much they enjoy their time off. Take a moment to think about that. A clue as to their level of happiness and success lies in the *frame of perception,* through which they view their job and their world. I shall not explain this particular point any further and urge you to take a few moments to meditate on the idea presented above.

I know some people who do nothing but complain about everything. I mean nothing is ever their responsibility and they're always complaining about being outdone somehow. Meeting them years later you may find that their conditions never changed even though they may have changed their job three or four times. If only they realized that the issue was within themselves and not external circumstances. They become victims of the vortex of their negative thoughts and are creating their own destinies through their habitual thoughts. There are others who move house every couple of years or change the furniture, the bathroom, the car every couple of months, but still never seem to be satisfied. Again the answer lies within themselves. It's not the room or furniture that needs changing, its their inner world and thoughts that need changing. They could change the furniture over and over again, yet until they realize this fact and sit down to consider, and understand the real root cause of their dissatisfaction.

There is wisdom in awareness and once you understand the causes and effects in a situation you can then set about changing the cause and thus the results.

It's All In Your Mind

Inject passion in your life. Don't go around in a kind of sleep walking depressed existence. Do something that will get the passion going in you. Visit a theme park, go carting, create and organise an inspiring event for charity, write a book. This miracle we call life is to be celebrated in every moment and every breath. How better to show your appreciation and thankfulness for this gift that God has given you than by, endeavouring to reach your higher potential and to help others to do the same. Think about it for a moment. How insulting it must be to God, if you do nothing but complain about life. That's as disappointing as giving someone a gift and watch them chuck it aside and not only avoid using it, but go around complaining about it. I truly hope that you see the point I'm making here. Don't wait around for some conditions to come about before you begin to conduct the great work on yourself and your life. Begin now. The way to WIN is to simply BEGIN. In this very moment, you can change your thoughts and therefore change the rest of your life. There is a saying that is almost worn out as a cliché, however it is imbued with truth. "Today is the first day of the rest of your life." I challenge you to go even further and to live each day as if it was the only day that exists. Don't think upon your past failure, understand that in the NOW, you are anything that you choose to think about. So forgive all trespasses and begin at once to live the life of love and passion and abundance that is your birthright.

You're the director so change the rest of the movie of your life to be whatever you would like it to be. You don't have to accept any previous limitations or hold yourself in the old mould that restrained you. Break the mould and create a new one, a better more positive one. If others resent the positive changes in you, realize that you have a choice as to how you react to that opinion, and your opinion is as valid as anybody else's and more valid in your life and situation.

The Importance of Forgiveness

Many ills and health problems that people experience are the result of harbouring hate for others and a desire to get even. It is very important to note the link between such negative thought and the impact it has on our health. We mentioned earlier that emotionalised thoughts attract similar thoughts to them and draw into your experience the object of those thoughts. Can you imagine for a moment, how destructive the habit of holding grudges and hate for the things that someone has done to you in the past. When you entertain such thoughts they can build up their own momentum and take on a life of their own and practically destroy an individual from the inside out. You are psychically linked to the object of your thoughts, so by continuing to seek revenge and think hateful thoughts against another, you are binding yourself to them and making yourself a psychological slave to the circumstance surrounding your relationship to them. That's easier said than done, I hear you say. It does take a certain degree of discipline to fully release and forgive a person that has hurt you or someone you know in the past. However, by your understanding of the mental laws, and your willingness to at least try, you will be exhilarated at the results that you get. People that have began to forgive those that have harmed them in the past, have found that many of their health problems have simply disappeared. Panic attacks soon subside, the constant throat infections seem to vanish and a whole list of benefits are recalled when one begins to exercise the act of forgiveness in their lives. Forgiveness does not mean that you go back to the old behaviours that allowed the other person to hurt you, but it is more a mental attitude that you hold to that person. What you actually do is release their hold on your inner thoughts and wish them well in their life. Understand that people are doing the best they can with the limitations of the experiences they have grown up with. So parents who show little affection for their children may have grown up in a family that have not demonstrated affection while they were a child, and they therefore do not have the social tools to provide or demonstrate the love and affection to their own children and so it goes. Of coarse, there are some that have had plenty and do know better and just seem to be vindictive in nature, but realize that nature is in no way vindictive and that something caused them to be the way they are.

The art of forgiveness is about releasing them with loving thoughts and holding no ill will against them. You may be assisted by reciting an affirmation such as,

"I release _____ from my life in love and wish him/her well, may God Bless _____ in all he/she does and I forgive him/her for what he/she has done in the past. The past is gone there is only the infinite NOW. The divine love of God radiates from me in all directions and strengthens me so."

You will be amazed at how liberating this is when you do it in a genuine way. If you simply grit your teeth and recite the words while, still thinking of how to exact your revenge, then you will not experience the benefits of true forgiveness. Immediately you should receive a confirmation from your Higher-Self in the form of a release of happiness and a rising sense of love in your life. Once again that which you give out shall come back to you. Think of others as you would like to have them think about you. If only more people understood the benefits and importance of forgiveness then human relationships would be infinitely improved.

Understanding.

One of the ways to achieve forgiveness is to seek understanding. Once you understand more about a person, culture or race then the barriers between you shall begin to fall, and set the way for more harmonious relationships. So many conflicts are born out of ignorance and fear. People will like and relate to you to the degree that you make them feel good about themselves. It is important to realize that we are all ONE, and we are all part of the divine being. Your mind is a part of and IS the ONE mind. You are a centre point in an infinite universe. Understanding banishes fear and makes us less susceptible to propaganda that encourages division and hatred amongst peoples. I believe that the more we learn about other people and educate ourselves in their ways, the more tolerance and harmonious shall be our interactions with them. So the next time you sense a loathing towards someone that you don't rightly know too well, make it your business to seek a fuller understanding of the individual. I recall that there was a quirky individual in my class in school, and he often displayed odd behaviours that the other kids did not quite understand, including myself. Then one day, somebody relayed to me the story of his family and how difficult his home life actually was. Let me tell you not only did I empathise with him, but with a little more understanding became far more tolerant of his unique behaviour. We live in a universe of cause and effect, and I urge you to make attempts to understand the cause, before passing judgement on the effect. People behave within the limitations of what they have learned and experienced so far. This principle applies on all levels. Understanding banishes fear. That is why therapies for overcoming all kinds of fears of animals seek to replace fearful ignorance with an understanding and knowledge of the thing itself. We fear the things that we don't know or understand.

Communication.

Learn and improve your language skills. Start your own library. Read voraciously. You can learn the strategies of any particular endeavour that you decide and commit to. Establish the habit of following through. Research your main area. Example. You may say that you know nothing of roses. But you can learn a lot even in an afternoon. Start by finding books on roses. Read as much as you can. Use the Internet to get images and latest research. And speak to people at garden centres about roses. Well as you can see within a very short time you will have a great deal of knowledge of roses. Action is what unites you to your outcomes. So, change I don't know to I will find out.

Communication is an area that offers wonderful opportunities for you to improve your life and the life of those that you encounter. To a great extent, how you get on in the world is determined by how you communicate with yourself, your internal talk, and how you communicate with the world around you. There is a constant streaming Mind TV inside your head. It is always on and the features of its programming are a representation of the experiences and memories of your life. Without your specific direction, the programs draw from those around you and from your environment. In the absence of disciplined imagination, the information is eclectic and flows and bends like leaves in the wind. If you do not direct these programs, they will direct you by default. They are fed by haphazard and often untrue beliefs, that you sucked in like a sponge throughout your life. The world within your mind is a miniature version of your life and the possibilities therein. Nothing manifests in the world without, that which manifests first in the mind within in the form of an idea and a thought. The first deed is thought, then the action and then the manifestation in reality. The very world in which we live in is a manifestation of God's great imagination. You are part of that creation and you are a part of God. When you realize this you will view the world in a different way and become infinitely more creative and align yourself with the forces of nature and spirit instead of running counter to them. You will flow more with the creative stream and find that circumstances and things will just fall into place. You will become a magus in the very sense of the word and create the life that you desire. But first comes the idea, the thought, and thoughts are things. First the world within, and then the world without, they are one and the same, an inseparable oneness. We are each a part of this oneness and as soon as we start being in the NOW and become internal architects we begin to build the world around us. All ideas, and great achievements and fortunes were first conceived as an idea in the mind of men and woman, each a part of the same infinite intelligence and infinite well of love. Choose wisely the thoughts that you entertain within, as they shall become the sum total of your mind. It is through concentration, focus and repetition that the thought becomes reality when fuelled by a burning desire and a faith to back it up. Getting back to the basic operating level of your mind or the day-to-day habitual thoughts that occupy the space in the garden of your mind. Root out negative thoughts, proclaim "get thee from my mind, and you shall no longer dwell in the sanctuary of my mind." Banish them and clear them from your garden as you would any intruder in the garden of your home that upsets the harmony and peace of your family. Then begin to plant the seeds of the very things that you want to manifest in your life. Know this, that if you fill your mind only with thought of things that you want, then you will most definitely attain them. It is an immutable law of mind and like other laws of nature, such as gravity it shall be as effective in creating good or ill, just as gravity may send a man to his death from a great height if he fails to work within its principles. When weeding the garden you will find old weeds that have started to grow many years before and have continued to stifle your success. They will resist leaving, and may be deep rooted, but you must be committed to removing them and not give in to their old patterns. It is not difficult to see this principle manifest itself even at the basic level, thus a man who's thoughts are messy and disorganised, inevitably has a dishevelled and disorganised life, his bedroom may be a mess, garden in a shamble, and appearance shabby and finances an even greater disaster. All these are mirror of the thoughts that he habitually maintains in the mind. The good thing is that change can be achieved in a moment. If the thoughts are changed in the world within then the conditions outside shall match that shift. The neurotransmitters of the brain shall animate his or her very being and behaviour to be consistent with the new set of beliefs. Once again it is a matter of what you choose to focus on. As much as possible we should aid ourselves to achieve the maximum results by working on all fronts, by being consistent all round. Also, by careful filtering and paying attention to the foods we eat, the images we pay attention to and the way we interpret the circumstances of ours lives. So the man that thinks himself stupid and had heretofore acted in a way consistent with that assumption, may at the drop of a hat be shown to be gifted and talented and with the right learning and attitude could excel to phenomenal levels well beyond what he or she may have ever thought possible. He may have previously accepted the idea, that he was stupid, and in the absence of any verifiable proof or adequate contradictory evidence, maintained this premise to be true. Proof can come about in the way of contradictory praise of the things that one has done well. As we said earlier that which we praise shall grow, and the qualities that we would like to see demonstrated in others should be praised if they are to be realized. The problem is that through cultural and environmental conditioning the old message can be deep seated. Like an inkblot on a clear white page, the fault becomes the focus and the potential of all that white space is ignored much to the detriment of the individual and their potential. So long as they focus on the black spot, they will miss all the magical glory of the white space around and the potential beyond. Such negative internal thoughts are extremely destructive and we should guard the gates of our mind vigilantly.

Stop validating these old behaviour patterns instead break them in. You may wrestle with them like a cowboy wrestles with a colt or wild stallion to break him in. A fierce battle ensues and then the power that was running wild and scattered is tamed and used to the benefit of the man who tamed it. Cast out negative beliefs from your mind by using the technique as per above. Change the major premise that has been acting as the blueprint of the operating manual of your mind. Throw away the old outdated thoughts, and choose a more empowering one that shall assist you in your goals. Think about it logically, and ask yourself "Is it more clever to apply these principles in my life and to use my automatic mind for my benefit, or to let it run on automatic taking me in all erratic directions and never finding a true path?" The question is loaded and implies the answer in itself, and it appeals to the reasoning side of your mind. This principle of the internal thoughts manifesting in outer reality, can be found throughout nature. The creative force of the universe manifests the objects of our desires. Many species of animals evolve and adapt to the needs appealed to their inner mind. The flying squirrels of Australia needed to fly, desired to fly, and after generations developed a skinned flange that allows them to soar between the treetops to find safety and food.

Humans on the other hand don't have to wait generations to manifest the objects that we desire. We don't have to wait generations for wings to manifest, as was the case with the squirrels. No instead, through the imaginative faculty of the mind, we have fashioned the materials around us and moulded our thoughts into solid reality, and built ourselves airplanes that allow us to fly around the entire planet in a matter of hours. The possibilities are endless and the limits we place on ourselves are set by the way we stifle our imaginative faculty. If set free, our imaginations can literally bring about practically any outcome that we can conceive. It is through the faculty of the imagination that we manifest our highest potential.

People who have achieved some of the most wonderful things in sporting history have done so by directing their thoughts to such an extend that they believed that they could not fail. For example the Olympic Athletes had won so many times in their inner minds, in their imaginings and visualizations, that when it came to the actual races they perform exactly as they imagined. They kept the image of what they wanted through all kinds of obstacles and environmental blocks. The fuel of desire and passion, persistence and self-belief drives them. In their inner mind, they visualise, affirm, and actually feel the sensations they would feel as they win the gold medal. When it comes to the event, they have the confidence to manifest the counterpart of their internal world. As within, so without! They are inverse thinkers to the negative patterns we talked about. They maintain the things that they want in their mind at all times, whereas the stifled and unsuccessful do the opposite and maintain the negative thoughts in their mind and even block out the positive. Recent research in sports psychology has shown that when athletes visualize the performances in their minds, that the physiology and neurotransmitters in the brain react as if they were physically practicing in reality. Then when they go to perform the task, they have the benefit of these many practice runs, and will perform as if they had practiced. Take note of this and ask yourself in what other areas can I mentally practice to increase my performance? I once read about a pilot who used to fly the bed, before any major flight exams. He actually performed all the tasks in his mind as he sat in bed, and when it came to the tests, he performed as if he had the benefit of hours of actual practice. Use this knowledge and practice tasks in your mind that you have to do. Very often top athletes that have used these principles have gone into the business world and used the same to reach the top of their field. You should get into the habit of practicing in advance. Do it as often as you think of it. Before your next business meeting, practice in your mind; imagine yourself doing well, and in as much details as possible. Use your personal magical trigger word as discussed earlier and go and perform the task as imagined, or as close as possible.

It's All In Your Mind

Once you get into the habit of doing this, it shall become built into your automatic success mechanism. Like many of the other techniques and principles outlined in this book, repetition and practice build habits and habits build your life. If you study the biographies of famous and influential people, you will find without exception these principles operating in their minds and thus in their lives. Break down the internal barriers, and your limits on what you can and will achieve and you shall begin at once to reach your higher potential.

It's All In Your Mind

Smile and the Whole World Smiles With You!

There is magic in laughter and in a smile. A couple of years ago a truck passed me on the island of Moorea, near Tahiti and in the back was a family with a young girl. The girl smiled as they passed and I could not help but smile back myself. That little Tahitian girl's smile has stuck with me ever since, it is lasting and its beauty had real power in it. Make it your business to smile a lot more. You will be amazed how much the world smiles with you. It is a vital piece of body language and a powerful force in our lives. When greeting people try to make the habit of smiling. I don't mean a cheesy grin, where possible try to foster a genuine ability to be happy to greet people. Let them see the beam their presence has on you. You will also notice that the people you seem to feel good around most are the ones that smile at you and show some signs of joy when they meet you. Making the habit of smiling is not only good for others but it is very good for your own well-being. The physiological act of smiling triggers electromagnetic activity in the brain relating to happiness. It reinforces the drive to smile and it will improve your human relationships immensely. Try it even for an afternoon. Smile more than you usually do. Do this even when greeting on the telephone, People will pick up the subtle thought vibrations in the tone of your voice. It is the silence between the words that carry the thoughts and create the atmosphere of the conversation. Pay as much attention to HOW you say things as you do to what you say. The very best communicators know how to change the tones of their voices to avoid causing conflict while at the same time getting their point across. Seek to make people feel comfortable and good about themselves in your presence. Take an earnest interest in the other person and make them the centre of your attention as they speak, and show an interest in what they have to say. This includes even if you do not agree with what they have to say, you can acknowledge their point of view. Do not invalidate it, or dismiss it as insane. You may acknowledge their point of view and then offer an alternative viewpoint. Remember that they are looking at things from their point of view; they see things through their perceptual goggles. That point of view may be far removed from yours, and the sooner you realize that everyone sees and experiences the world in their own unique way, then you will be far more understanding in your dealings with others. It is a kind of agreeing to disagree if you will. I like to call it communication Aikido. Of coarse there will be occasions when you need to assert your point of view stronger than at other times, but in the majority of occasions you will improve your communication with others if you do not invalidate what they say. Treat their Ego's like a balloon and your words like a pen writing on that balloon, if you press too hard you will burst their bubble. But if you make your point with a good degree of firmness and work around the circumference of the balloon you can still get you words across it without taking the wind out of another.

The older sister of smiling is laughter and you should do as much of it as you can possibly do in your life. Read funny articles, rent comedies, and generally have a laugh with your friends, work colleagues, and family. It is very good for you, and when you laugh your emotional mechanism in the brain releases the feel good hormones and your whole body radiates after a good laugh. It can literally cure the sick. A well-documented case was that of Norman Cousins, who had been diagnosed with an incurable disease and was given a certain amount of time to live. So what did he do, he decided not to believe in the doctor's timeframe and went out and rented as many comedies as he could find, and read funny books and literally laughed himself well. He recovered fully much to the surprise of the medical doctors. So go on have a laugh, you will feel much better for it, and so will those around you.

The Secret of Living is Giving.

The way to receive something is to give it. If you want to receive more love, you need to give more love. If you want to receive more wealth you should give away a certain amount of your own money. That's right, give it away and not loan it out at interest or hold it against someone to whom you give. By the act of giving you will set about a powerful circular force that will eventually return to you multiplied.

That which you try to hold on to tightly shall slip from your hands as sand does when you try to hold onto it as tightly as possible. Try it the next time you are at the beach. Pick up a fistful of sand and clasp your hand as tight as you can and note how quickly the grains slip away from you. The same is true of money matters. Be prepared to give away a certain amount of your income, and by doing so you create a sense of abundance within yourself that states to your subconscious mind that there is such abundance that we can help others as well. Your powerful subconscious will begin to find more ways to fill the vacuum that you have created and resources shall come to you from areas that you may never have expected. Not to mention the effect that it will have on those whom benefit from your generosity. You should give a tithe of your income to help others and to keep the flow of wealth running through you like a siphon. Imagine yourself as a siphon from a great endless and infinite lake. Once you give you create the initial vacuum that starts the water to flow through the tube and by continuing to give you will continue to receive. When you stop giving you block the tube and the siphon no longer draws from the source until you start the process again. Once again in order for the process to be truly effective you should give in the spirit of generosity and not with a condition that you demand something back from those you give, that would take the good out of it and reduce the effect and benefit for all concerned. Be generous, don't be tight with money or you will always experience lack. It can be as simple as buying someone lunch when the opportunity arises, demonstrate your willingness to give and you will soon begin to feel the abundance. Very often they will reciprocate your generosity on other ways. Psychologically you will feel the benefits too. You will derive a sense of joy in helping others and it is health for you to begin to get a sense of the infinite abundance that exists all around us. Other ways you may give is to give a certain amount to charities and the needy. This will result in your labour and talents blessing others as well as yourself. If you don't have much money just give what you can. Unless you experience this concept it is difficult to understand, but give it a try and you will soon be counting the blessings that you pour on others and that others shall pour on you. Start the siphon flowing and give and never stop giving. It doesn't just have to be money. You may give of your time and help someone out; you may volunteer to help out at a society that helps the less fortunate. Above all give of your love, demonstrate your love of God and humanity by acting in accordance with that love. One way to do it is by serving. It is a principle that built the massive corporations all over the world. Serve others and you shall prosper.

Section 2

Harnessing The Hidden Power Of Your Mind

"Your body is like a robe that cloaks your thoughts" Noel Cox

The Power of Focus and Concentration

There are few subjects that will reward you as well as the study of the science of mind and spirit. For they contain the immutable laws of nature and achievement. Within its grasp is the very process of creation. Our objective in this life is to create. We are by our nature creative beings. There are riches all around us and man is only beginning to understand the universe about him. Even in this age we still have but an inkling of an understanding of the processes of the brain. Esteemed Yale psychologist, William James, estimated that we use only 10% of our brain's capacity. I would say that this is a conservative figure and it is becoming apparent now that our brains functioning may very well be infinite. There are literally billions of cells in the human brain, and the more we use our brains the more they develop. Studies have shown that brains actually change physiology when we learn new tasks. Each experience we have changes us for better or worse. It is estimated that our brain can remember everything in our lifetime, billions of pieces of information. Recent studies have indicated that our memories may be perfect in that under the right conditions we may even recall every detail of an experience or event from the distant past. You may have had the odd experience of a past dream rising in your memory and everything in it is clear to you in that instant. Certain smells may conjure up memories of someone or places of long ago, of which you had not thought of for years. Experiments at Duke University by Dr. Joseph Banks Rhine, have proved statistically that our minds may affect matter, and sense thoughts or events outside of the normal five senses. So it is a strange occurrence that with the most advanced Bio-computer in the universe inside our skulls that so many people are barely surviving let alone thriving on the basis of its understanding. It was as if we have been given the most powerful piece of equipment, only to let it lie dormant without using it to reach our higher potential. It is a divine gift. So this book shall serve as a user manual for unlocking some of the secrets of your mind. In so doing you will find yourself being and doing things far beyond what you thought possible. Remember that knowledge is only potential power, unless it is put to use. So you need to take action and implement the techniques and methods in order for them to have any significant effect on your life.

Your brain consists of two parts, a left and a right brain. Each of the performs different functions and the left brain controls the logical functioning such as numbers, words, verbal skills, language Etc. and your right brain is where you process colour, imagination, spatial awareness, music. One of the keys to increasing your brainpower is to balance or stimulate both brain hemispheres in order to enhance your ability to perform tasks.

A secret that had been maintained by the mystics and masters of the past in order to protect it from getting into the hands of the unsound and unbalanced has recently come into public light. If understood it can work wonders in the lives of people and helps us all to reach our higher potential. It is so simple that even when presented to people it is still not understood for its magical and transformational capacity. Many will read these words and gloss past it as superficial or oversimplified nonsense, but a certain number of people who are ready for its message and eternal truth shall benefit greatly and so shall those around them. If even one individual gains a clearer understanding of the principle, then the work of these words shall have been worth it. It is contained in one sentence and when you read it I want you to stop and think about it for a couple of moments. The great secret is;

Everything in your life is determined by the thoughts that you think.

Please stop and read the sentence again. Now let me explain in clear and practical terms what this means.

In psycogological terms we are thinking and holding conversations with ourselves in every moment. Even when you are performing mundane tasks your mind is wandering on past, future or present events and a conversation is taking place within your mind. This may be likened to a stream of images, or our own life movie. It is always playing, even when we are asleep. It is this process that creats the very conditions and experiences in our lives. This is merely the surface of the spring in terms of our awareness of how this creates the way we live our life. Einstein's Theory of Relativity states that energy and matter are one and the same. That energy may be changed into matter and that matter may be changed into energy. Another law of physics states that energy cannot be created or destroyed it can only be changed from one form to another. Hence, when you pull the brakes on your bicycle the kinetic energy is transformed into heat energy by the friction of the brake pad on the wheel rim, and the velocity is changed into heat and the bicycle comes to a stop. Now brain waves are a form of energy too and your thoughts are part of your brainwaves. *These thoughts are things.* Thought energy is what animates your body in a certain way. When you think a thought, an electromagnetic signal is sent through your nervous system and results in the movement of your muscles and an action takes place. Every cell in your body responds to your every thought. Subjects under hypnosis have manifested blisters in the place where the hypnotist has placed a harmless pen and suggested it was a hot poker. It was the belief of the individual that the suggestion made was true that resulted in the signal being sent to the cells in the area touched. It is possible to think yourself sick. This truth is applicable to everything in your life. For example, what you think about will determine what you do and say, which results in how you experience life in general. You may spend your time worrying and thinking about bills or persons or situations, and this is manifested in your every move and in your body. Understand that your brain cannot tell the difference between a real or imagined experience, and when you think and worry about things it manifests in your body in the form of a stress reaction, just as the blister manifested in the above example. Your mind responds with releasing stress hormones to deal with the imagined situation.

That Which You Focus Your Attention on Grows in Your Experience and Life.

When you focus your attention on a specific thing, you are giving power and control to that thing. So you may be in debt and all you can think about all day long is about the growing credit balance and your concerns thereof. Hence your subconscious mind takes up the signal and brings those conditions into effect in your life, albeit by the thoughts you think and the actions you take.

There are physical implications in the premise that *Thoughts are Things.* The whole universe consists of energy. You are an energy being, constantly giving off energy in the form of sound, heat, electromagnetism motion etc. In a sense we are ONE with the universe and with everything. Even the seemingly solid objects and matter are really only energy moving at different vibrations. The book you are holding, chairs, rocks all matter is really only energy vibrating at different frequencies, with moving electrons protons and neutrons, and not really solid in the smaller scales. Mystics believe that the universe is part of God's imagination and that the divine is in all of us. You are a divine being and a part of God. In a true sense we ARE all ONE. Dr. Joseph Banks Rhine proved as far as statistically possible the impact of focused thought on inanimate objects such as the role of a dice. His methods had been scrutinised to a point of exhaustion and the evidence he presented good enough to convince even the most hardened sceptics.

You have the ability to start to control your thoughts in a habitual way so that you may manifest your truest desires in your life. It is absolutely vital to only focus on the things that you want and keep them off the things that you do not want. We shall work on directing your thoughts in a more empowering way and to begin to use this force for you instead of allowing it to work against you. The good news is that the methods are as simple as the above truths. Do not be fooled by there simplicity, as they shall create magic in your experience.

It's All In Your Mind

Affirmations and Visualizations.

You can turn on the miracle working power of your mind by way of affirmations and creative visualization. These are the best way to impress your wants and desires to your subconscious mind and to set in motion the creative force that will bring them into your reality. You are using these tools all the time, but most likely in a haphazard and automatic way. By the negative self talk and the images that you have been holding in your head on a habitual basis, you have been creating your life as it is. *I think, therefore I am.* From now on you are going to learn effective ways of taking control of this infinitely creative force that you have been given and to use it for your benefit and the benefit of others. You and your life are the sum total of all your thoughts and feelings to date. Everything in your life has resulted from your way of thinking and the decisions you have made before now. If you continue to do and think what you have always done then you will always get the same results. Change your way of thinking and you change your life.

A simple and effective way of doing this is by giving clear unambiguous instructions to your subconscious mind, or as I like to term it your inner crew. It helps to imagine that you are the *director* of a movie crew and they need clear instructions, a script and a clear image of that which you want. If you pass this information on to your inner cast and crew they will make the movie of your life consistent with those thoughts. If you speak to them about how you can't do certain things or cannot have certain things the crew or your subconscious mind takes these as truth statements and create these conditions in your reality. There is one member of the cast that you need to keep in check and that is the main actor or protagonist called the ego. He or she will need to be spoken to in a fair, but firm manner if you are to keep control of the set and how the movie progresses. Just as a movie director would have to gain the cooperation of a movie star in a large production. Sometimes the actor and director may differ slightly in opinions on how to proceed. In like manner you may wish to direct your life in a certain way only to have the ego rise to the surface and protest that it is not consistent with your self-image to that point. Speak to yourself, and your inner crew in a way that is firm but fair. That way it is clear that you are in the director's chair, the seat of the will if you like.

All day long an image and auditory stream are playing in your head. You may think of it as a kind of MTV or Inner Mind Television. Your inner stream is on 24 hours and feeds on the content on the previous thoughts you hold about yourself and all your experiences up to now. A surprising amount of it may be negative and has been conditioned that way since childhood. All you have to do is listen to how parents talk to their children in a supermarket to notice how such negative programming takes place at an early stage. You will most likely witness a barrage of firm and negative statements, such as "No we can't afford that", "Put that back you're always so bold." Nearly always it contains, *can't*, *no*, and dangerous generalizations such as *always*. The impressionable mind of the child picks these things up and a neurological link takes place in the mind between the conditions and the statement, thus a circle of poverty can begin to take route.

The way to start taking control of this inner stream is to begin to substitute the old programs for new more effective ones that are consistent with what you want. All you need is a pen and paper, and a desire to use your imagination in a directed way. Affirmations are basically a statement that you write or say to yourself in order to impress the content on your higher mind. It is like scratching out the old grooves of a record and replacing it with a clear and static free DVD. There are some guidelines that should be followed when using affirmations so as to derive the maximum benefit.

Affirmations should,

1. Be clear and specific.
2. Be stated in the present tense, in the eternal NOW.
3. They should be said with feeling and emotion.

Here is an example of the differing kinds of affirmations that you use. Remember that your inner crew and higher mind are always listening to your self talk and taking it at face value so use this knowledge to your own advantage.

Examples of positive affirmations are,

"I am happy, calm and confident in all situations."

"I am a confident and happy University Lecturer. I enjoy passing on profound knowledge to my students."

"Every day in every way I am getting better, better and better."

"Everyday in every way I am getting richer, richer and richer."

You may also reinforce it with a second directional affirmation, which is from a different angle.

"Noel (your name) is a confident and happy University Lecturer. Noel enjoys passing on profound knowledge to students"

Personal directed affirmation,

It's All In Your Mind

"Noel you are a confident and happy University Lecturer. Noel you enjoy passing on profound knowledge to your students."

Try each of them out for yourself and design your own. It is very important to add the feeling and emotion element when saying it. It is like the electricity that charges a magnet. So take a deep breath and key yourself up, raise your physical body as you would when you are excited and speak to yourself in a convincing tone. Once again I must repeat, for I do not want you to forget that the feeling of excitement and expectancy is the key ingredient to affirmations otherwise they are wandering prayers with no potency, as weak as Superman in the presence of kryptonite. You may be thinking that this stuff is a load of cobbler's nonsense. Look, don't worry I know how you feel, I felt the same way and then I realized that it was worth a shot. The truth is that your mind is infinitely powerful and creative. You are actually creating with each of your thoughts, and the words and images you hold in your mind have wondrous power, that only through experiencing you may really appreciate the effectiveness of these techniques. You can only gain by trying. If you don't add the FEELING element, it is like baking apple tart without the apples. How may I create this so called feeling, I simply don't feel excited so what am I supposed to do? I understand that sentiment too, so with a little understanding of the mind body relationship you will begin to develop the effectiveness of creating this feeling. As mentioned a few moments ago, you can key yourself up by your physiology. What you do in your mind effects the things you do in your body, and vice versa. If you smile then there is a resultant response in the brain that triggers a little highway of neurological activity that heightens your feeling of joy. It is much more difficult to feel down while you have a gleaming smile across your face. That's a false, ridiculous smile, I feel silly you say. Don't worry if it does not come comfortably to you at the start. The objective is not for you to force yourself, you should enjoy these techniques in a playful way. So to begin to key your body up you should sit or stand up straight and take a deep breath and hold a picture of the thing you want in your mind. Then affirm to yourself in as excited a manner as you can the statement that you have prepared. The FEELING element of the affirmation will draw the message to the deeper levels of your mind with the tag, (s)he's serious about this one, we better produce this result for the director, or captain. Then as you go about your daily business your powerful subconscious shall be creating and directing you to the circumstances and things that are closer to your main aim. The following is a very useful way of using affirmations to change the quality of your life.

The Secret Path to Success

The following is a simple guideline to the stages to reaching your outcome.
1. Know what you want
2. Desire it hard enough
3. Have faith, belief and expectancy that it will happen..
4. Be persistent towards attaining it and learn from your outcomes.
5. Be willing to pay the price for its attainment
6. Understand and believe that you are guided and directed by the Universal Life Force, a higher power and express your appreciation that it is so.

It's All In Your Mind

One of the most effective ways to demonstrate your faith that something will be so is to give thanks to God before you receive it. It truly works. You may also reinforce this by recalling times from your past when so-called coincidences came to serve you well. Concentrate upon them and use them as proof references.

It's All In Your Mind

1. Know What You Want

Overcome the problem of inertia.

In some respects the laws of mind reflect the laws of physics and one such case is the law of inertia. A body at rest is more difficult to move than a body already in motion. Anyone that has ever pushed a car will understand this principle clearly. It takes a great effort to get the car moving from rest and to get it going, but once it is moving its own momentum contributes to the movement and it is easier to keep it going. The mind has a similar problem in that a person can become habitually lazy or settle into a comfort zone of inactivity. They may associate more pain to doing something than remaining where they are. It takes an initial push to start the ball rolling. Understand the influence that this principle may be holding over you. By being aware of it you are on your way to knowing how to overcome it. The way to overcome it is to stack the odds in your favour. The idea is to imagine what doing nothing is costing you in your life. Take time to think about it. Then on the other hand imagine what you could achieve if you took action. You may prefer to write down your lists and stack the items under each heading. Understand that life is a gift and should be lived to the full, figure out exciting things that you would like to do and achieve. You need to find direction in your life to make you want to move, what you need to do is set inspiring goals.

Momentum

Momentum is a force that builds in proportion to the amount of action taken and the desire behind it. The more momentum you build up, the more potent the degree of force exerted. Learn to operate with momentum in tasks that you undertake, focus and concentrate on the completion of the tasks and the activities with which you are engaged. Many actors have commented on the force and speed with which Steven Spielberg directs movie scenes. Some said that they found it hard to believe that scenes could be directed with such speed and accuracy. When asked about it Spielberg simply stated that you can't loose momentum, or boredom sets in and this effects the energy of the whole crew. So he manages to keep the whole cast and crew mobilised and doing something at all times. Do not overlook the importance of this principle. It is a formidable force in getting things done. This very force has won battles, and the sheer momentum of the attacking force has overcome armies. Keep on taking action towards your goals, and become a supreme doer. Don't rest on your laurels. Think of great people throughout history, and realize that they had the same 24 hours each day that you have. Yet they achieved so much. See yourself as a steam train heading for a goal or destination. Gain momentum and feel the energy building up inside you. This is the building of the desire force, stoked by the will. Your desire is the hot steam and your Will directs to drive the system forward. Increase your speed and efficiency in doing things and make it your new *modus operandi*. Lists and goals are essential aids to the Will in directing this powerful energy.

It's All In Your Mind

Goal Setting

A tourist and an Irishman were standing at a bus stop in Dublin. A bus zipped past with no name or number on it. Puzzled the tourist asked, "Where is it going?" The Irishman turned with a smile and said, "my friend it's going nowhere fast."

Don't be like a bus with no number or destination, know exactly where you are going and others will step on board and go along with you.

One of the greatest hindrances to success is not knowing what you want to be or where you want to go. You cannot hit a target that you cannot see. You may ask any number of people exactly what they want to be and almost nine out of ten will give you vague answers and show that they have no direction at all. Expecting success, riches and your soul mate to arrive at your doorstep is a bit like placing a blindfold on, spinning around in a room and hoping to hit the bull's-eye with a dart. You most get out there and make things happen for yourself. Often focussed concentration and thought is enough to bring you the ideas that will bring you all you want in life. But first you must seek,

"So I say to you, ask, and it will be given you; search, and you will find; knock, and the door will be opened for you. /10/ For everyone who asks receives, and everyone who searches finds, and for everyone who knocks, the door will be opened.
Luke 11:9-10

The most beneficial thing that you can do is to sit down and spend some time deciding exactly what it is you want. So many people go through their life without ever doing this in a scientific or practical way. It should be the first thing that people are taught how to do in schools as far as I'm concerned. Our minds are goal seeking by design. It is that insatiable urge built into man to strive and do more. It is in you and you must find a channel for it. You have a mind that can produce all that you ever could imagine. It may be likened to a powerful boat in a harbour with a crew at the ready, waiting to take you to anywhere in the world. You are the captain of this boat. What you have been doing up to now has been similar to setting the boat in motion and taking your hand off the wheel and letting it hit any obstacle that it comes across and eventually if left long enough it may end up on the rocks or sunk. You have given no instruction to the crew and they are not permitted to do anything without your orders and watch in dismay and disappointment as you have been allowing the vessel to become shipwrecked. Now that you realize that you are the boat's captain and responsible for the vessel and its crew, you may begin to plan exactly where you would like to take it. The crew of your vessel, your subconscious, are ordered to follow every single command that you give, so it is important that you give them clear instructions and a clear image and plan of where the vessel is to be taken. I hope this example shall help you to realize that you really are in command of the vessel of your life and that you are "The Captain of thy soul, the of … thy destiny."

Now what we are going to do is take control of the wheel and give the crew the clear instructions they need. A piece of advice that I would have is, that very often when you hit the truth of something that you are going to do, the crew and your higher self will celebrate and you may feel the enthusiasm and excitement rush through your whole body. This is your intuition telling you that what you have chosen or thought about is right for you. Eternal truths have the ability to cause this reaction in you. Many of the concepts in this book will ring true to you and your higher self will recognise them for what they are. Embrace the moment and realize that this is the birth of desire and nature's fuel shall place the wind in the sails of the vessel and move it along.

Like other tasks you need to associate the pleasure of setting the goals in order for you to feel sufficiently enthusiastic enough to go ahead and spend the time doing it. I urge you to do this and not to simply pass it over. This is a vital action signal to your subconscious mind that you're serious about your plans. I had come across this concept a good few years ago and was amazed to find that when I returned to my list a couple of years later, that all the items had been checked off as accomplished. It is a part of the magical processes of the mind, and a small price to pay for the results that it achieves. I had set a list to see many of the world's tropical islands, and even wrote down a list of the exact places. At the time of writing the list I had no means or no idea of how I could possibly get there. Sure enough within a surprisingly short period of time, one by one the magical concepts in this book took me to Bermuda, Hawaii, Mauritius, Seychelles, and Tahiti, Fiji…and even in First Class. I have returned to these islands a number of times and owe the absolute joyous experiences to the principles and techniques that I hereby outline in this book. I am confident that they will bring you on a similar magical journey that they have brought me and possibly far better.

It's All In Your Mind

Let's place the hand on the wheel and get the image in mind of exactly what it is you want. In order to decide where you want to go, it is a good idea to get an orientation of your current position and to know how far you have to go. All journeys start at a beginning point and end at a destination. If you feel disheartened with your current situation, do not despair because this is good feedback. If you did not feel this sense of want for something more, you would be happy being exactly where you are and would not feel the need to try to make changes in your life. Like all other feedback, thank it for its message and do something about it. In that way you are giving feedback to your higher faculty and acknowledging its message. When you do this, it will reward you with other aid in achieving that which you set out to achieve. Congratulations, you have a desire to change and that's good news. You need to decide exactly what you want to be and do.

Use a pen and paper to jot down your ideas. You may keep jotting down as many ideas as you desire and keep the pen moving. Keep an image in mind of all the things that you would like to have in your life and all the things you would like to do. Tip, do not restrict your imagination jot down any ideas that you may have as desires in your mind. Do not fail to put them down because you think they are unrealistic. Nothing is impossible to those that believe and have faith. Indulge yourself, whatever you dream of doing...travel to Hawaii around the world...to own a Mercedes Benz. Write all your ideas down and keep that pen moving, you may have things like, travelling the world, marrying a kind, caring and attractive person, having happiness, a nice home and financial independence. These are just some of the ideas that you may be putting down but there are an infinite amount that you may feel free to add. Don' be embarrassed about any of your goals because they are yours to achieve and yours alone. By all means keep this list completely private and don't share it with others if you feel that they will not support you in an encouraging way. Too many talented people have dropped their dreams in a whim because of some ridicule and laughter from others. This is between you, your higher self, and God.

In order to give you some direction and to help you get some balance in the goals that you set. The following is a suggested list of headings for your goals.

Business/Career Goals
Financial/Money Goals
Family Goals
Contribution Goals
Relationship Goals
Leisure/Travel/Adventure Goals
Education and Personal Development Goals.

Now that you have a good list of goals under each of the above headings. You should write them down in a list under, 1 year goals, 3 year goals, and 5 year goals. Place them under each heading and note how many ideas that you have.

What you are going to do next is check them for consistency. One of the big mistakes that people can make when setting goals is that they set two inconsistent goals in motion, and goals that tug in different directions. What you need to do is check your list for things that are not taking you in the same direction and are inconsistent with each other. In those instances you need to decide which one is more important to you and then get rid of the one that is less important or desirable to you between the two. You need to be ruthless in this case as if you do not; you will set your vessel off to reach a goal only to realize that the tug rope from an incompatible one is holding you to the dock. Make your goals as compatible and consistent as possible. In addition to this you need to make sure that they are compatible with your self-image also or the self-image of whom you want to be. Make your goals in line with truth and honesty. The forces of nature that come into play with goal setting should only be used to the greater good of human kind. Do not set goals that are not good towards your fellow man. Nature has implemented a law that would eventually return the bad turns on you and you will get what you give out.

That is an important law and you should remember it.

You get back what you give out.

Now that you have your list of goals in mind and on paper. They should all be compatible and consistent with each other and with the new you. You should now begin an imagination exercise and that is to imagine that you are living the goals as they are listed. Visualize them in a relaxed state in as much details as you possibly can. Actually see and feel yourself in the situation in your mind's eye. If it is a wonderful house, smell the wood floors and hear the creaking of the wood in the doors and look out your window at that sea view. Enjoy the experience in the now as much as possible. Write out this list of goals and incorporate them in your perfect day in that time in the near future.

Break down the goals to daily tasks, and do not let a day go by without having done something towards reaching your goal. This is important. If you find that you do not have a lot of time, resolve to do a little. It is better to do a little often than nothing at all. In most cases when you set down to achieve a small achievable goal, you tend to take the necessary action to do it. If you set down to do a larger amount, sometimes the task will appear too great and you will associate more pain with doing it than not doing it.

Your Success Collage

An effective way to help your mind hold a clear image of that which you want is to make yourself a Success Collage. All you do is get a blank piece of paper or if you like and are more technically minded you may do it on an image application on your computer. Collect a serious of pictures that represent as best as possible your goals and aspirations. Cut out pictures from magazines and newspapers of the exact things that you would like. Get some sticking paste and paste them on the piece of paper. I recommend that you join the images by a serious of lines, and that it have a sequential flow to it. If you want to write a book first and covet a prize, you could cut out a picture of the edge of a book and the logo for the booker prize. Then after that if you wanted to have a car, paste a picture of your dream car, be specific make sure it is the make and colour that you desire. You may place anything on there that your heart desires. Then the best place to put this is near your bed where you can focus your attention on it before going to bed and upon waking in the morning. Many people have found this to work magic in their life and the things that they had placed in their list of goals and on their success collage have materialised in the most unexpected ways.

2. Desire It Hard Enough

Desire! Nature's Fuel

In order to make you feel like taking action it is vital that you desire a thing strong enough. It is a strong desire that will magnetise you to that which you want. It is not enough to simply know what you want, but you must want it enough to do the things necessary to attain it. In order to come through the inevitable obstacles the will be in your way both internally and externally you need a burning desire for the thing. If you do not have a burning all consuming desire for the thing in your mind, then you may be swayed and falter before the slightest piece of resistance.

If you study the interviews or the biographies of any successful man or woman, you will find a common thread and that is they desired the thing they do so much that they had an all-consuming passion. This all consuming passion made them oblivious to the many set backs and obstacles that had come there way. Many had started out with tremendous disadvantages. Beethoven was deaf?

A burning desire more often than not starts off with a spark of inspiration and the thought seed grows in the mind of the individual until he or she becomes magnetised to it. Like thoughts attract like thoughts and soon the person finds that they begin to find themselves doing things and in situations consistent with their major goals. It doesn't matter what your current situation is, you have the capability of reaching your goal. A burning desire to reach a specific objective pulls at the very fabric of the universe to help you attain that which you set out to achieve.

"The moment one definitely commits oneself, then providence moves too. All sorts of things occur to help one that would never otherwise have occurred. A whole stream of events issues from the decision, raising in one's favour all manner of unforeseen incidents and meetings and material assistance which no man could have dreamed would have come his way. Whatever you can do or dream you can, begin it. Boldness has genius power and magic in it. Begin it now."
Goethe

Realize that nature will not place in man a desire that he cannot achieve. God always places the means to achieving a goal along with the goal itself. It is desire that helps fuel action. Stoke the fire of desire within you to reach your goals. In order to demonstrate the power of desire, a teacher took a student of his out in a boat and was giving him a lesson. The boy asked, what was the secret to success? The teacher looked at him and pushed him over board. The boy struggled to climb back in the boat, but his teacher merely grabbed his head and pushed him under water. The boy struggled and struggled for breath. Eventually he let the boy back in the boat when. The boy dismayed, asked what was that about. The teacher responded, "When you were under water, what did you desire most of all?" The boy answered, "to breathe, I wanted to breathe most of all and it was the only thing on my mind." Then the teacher said, "If you desire something as you desired to breathe when under the water, nothing shall stop you from achieving it. That is the secret of success"

It's All In Your Mind

A genuine desire for a thing makes the person irresistible to it. A psychic link is set up and the more the person thinks upon and visualizes the attainment of the object of his or her desire the quicker it will come to them.

The brother of desire is the will. The will complements desire in everyway. If desire is the fuel in a car, the will is the control, the steering wheel, the gears and the pedals. It is the will that is the directing force that channels the desire force in the direction of what you want. The will is the mould into which you pour the cement of desire and create the masterpieces in your life. People of strong will power make their mark in the world. To exert the will to a definite end when keyed up with desire can create miracles and make you an unstoppable force. In simple terms the will is demonstrated in an individual who decides upon a coarse of action and commits to its completion no matter what the obstacles. A strong willed person will not be drawn away by distractions and scatter his or her energies in different directions. Instead, a person of will focuses and concentrates on their goal at all times and continues to take action until it is achieved. The magnetic force of desire draws you to your dreams, your will controls and directs this force and ensures that you reach your desired destination. The way to develop this willpower is to become one pointed. Think upon that which you desire as often as you can and discipline yourself to a degree that the majority of your actions and your energy are going towards reaching your goal. Desire provides the feeling and emotional energy and the will channels this energy into a laser beam that is electromagnetic and shall bring the circumstances of your desire into reality. The motive force of the will is complementary to the emotional force of your desire and together create any conditions in your life that you could ever want. Become decisive, learn to focus and concentrate on achieving your goals, and stick with it until it is complete. Successful people in different fields of work seem to demonstrate this understanding without even consciously thinking about it. The scholar spends many hours concentrating on his or her studies, and commits to the completion of the coarse work to the exclusion of the many distractions such as TV, or going to the bars, that the less successful people tend to fall prey to. They scatter their energies in all different directions, and thus are less effective.

In order to demonstrate to Nature that you deserve your outcome, you must,

It's All In Your Mind

3. Have Faith, Belief and Expectancy That It Will Happen.
"And he marvelled at their unbelief" Mark 6.6

So Jesus said to them, "Because of your unbelief; for assuredly, I say to you, if you have faith as a mustard seed, you will say to this mountain, 'Move from here to there,' and it will move; and nothing will be impossible for you." Matthew 14: 14-21

One thing that is a common message from all the world's religions is that we must have faith and belief in order to create miracles in our life. Jesus said that we could move mountains if we only believed wholeheartedly. A person magnetised by belief can literally create miracles. There are thousands of documented healings from around the world from people who by their faith had healed themselves or received healings from others. I know of a lady who had been diagnosed with a form of lung cancer and had been sent home to die with merely pain control. She prayed in earnest to Padre Pio and believed without reservation in his intersession and merciful healing, and within days she was completely cured. Upon returning to the hospital a while later they were amazed to see such a recovery. Jesus himself healed the blind and the sick, and preached that we all could do this if we only believed. Our own subconscious is infinitely powerful and once directed with clarity and belief can achieve anything. It is the same God given power that heals the cut in your finger within a matter of hours and restores cells to there previous state. It is a fact that every cell in your body is replaced every eleven months. From a physical standpoint your body is really only eleven months old. What holds it all together is the life force mould of your powerful subconscious mind. Our brains and our body are electromagnetic. The air we breathe has electromagnetism in fact everything is electromagnetic. Once you realize that you are one with the universe and understand that your thoughts can affect matter even at a distance. If you know how to use it, your mind can become a conductor and influencer of this very powerful force and can be used towards the good of your fellow beings. If a person is to achieve anything of note, he or she must believe that they can achieve it, otherwise what would be the point of even trying. It was the magnificent power that allowed one gentle loving little man to dispel a powerful empire from his country and empower over 400,000,000 Indian people to take their fate back into their own hands. His name, Mahatma Gandhi. One must fill his cup of belief before he can make others believe too. It was with absolute faith and belief, and unwavering courage that Mahatma Gandhi performed the almost impossible. Impossible, the one word that man must dispel from his spoken usage. Too many people spurt it out in a flurry anytime something challenging is mentioned. This cuts off the faith power that makes anything possible to the believer. You must believe in yourself as well as the thing that you set out to achieve. Cultivate self-confidence and instil its virtue in your every activity. Believe yourself capable of doing anything and you are. "According to your faith, it is done unto you"

Build the habit of faith in yourself. Recall times when you done something that you're proud of and use them as references for your ability. You are a Divine Being and are made up of the very stuff of the universe and have been given dominion over the energy of all things. Become aware that you are operating at far less than you are capable of doing and through the power of your mind can do all things that you desire. "If God be for you, then who can be against you"

God is in each of us and if we pray in the correct way can achieve miracles in our lives. It is important to direct your power only towards the betterment and love of mankind if you are to be a channel of the power that is lifeward. If you try to use it for wicked purposes it will be cut off from you and any ill you wish on others shall boomerang back on you as per the spiritual law of correspondence.

When you begin to believe in the science of mind and spirit, it shall begin to reveal to you its secrets to you. In terms of the spirit realm, believing is seeing. I had once been a so-called materialist, and only believed that what I saw in the physical world about me. Anything else was laughable nonsense. When I began to read about the science of mind and spirit, and suspended judgement for a time, the strange secrets began to reveal themselves to me. The first time I experienced clairvoyance on a personal basis it was so clear to me at the time, I drew a sketch with the odd characteristics of the image and dated it before later finding it to be exact in every detail. It was a flash in the mind that left no doubt as to its nature. Truth has a way of impressing itself clearly within you. It strikes resonance with an inner knowing. It all sounds a little quirky right, well if its any comfort to you it took me a while to come to terms with the new reality too. It strikes me as odd too that so many that go to mass every week and pray tend then cringe at the mere mention of the spirit realm. Maybe they think the priest is just having a laugh or doing it for the good of his health of something. Understand that we are multi dimensional beings. What does that mean, well it means that we are a trilogy in one. We are made up of mind, body and spirit. We operate and are influenced by each of these realms. In fact they are merely separated by vibrational frequency and the power of faith and belief can bring forth the object of your thoughts into physical reality.

First it is registered as a thought in the mind.

It exists as an image or energy in the spirit realm and is brought forth into the physical by a process of focus and concentration on the desired outcome. It is conducted through the nature of your thoughts and the more feeling and emotion they have the more electromagnetism they have to create that which is desired and to magnetise or draw you to those things. The third stage is to take physical action.

Faith can be developed by using affirmations mixed with feelings repeated to your subconscious mind. You may foster the faith power by reading aloud an affirmation of your desired outcome with as much feeling as you can muster. Then give thanks for it already having been achieved.

It's All In Your Mind

Belief and the Placebo Effect.

The placebo effect is a medical phenomenon that has been studied around the world. It is based on the power of belief and when a person is given a tablet with non medicinal properties whatsoever, and told by a doctor or whomever that it is a remedy for the illness suffered by the patient, then the patient tends to recover as per the suggested properties of the tablet. In fact the tablet may be a mere sugar tablet. Patients have had pain relief and miraculous healings based on the suggested benefits of the tablet being ingested. In some test cases two groups of people had been separated both groups requiring knee surgery to heal a painful knee complaint. Both groups had been separated and the ritual of surgery carried out on both groups of patients. The surgeon entered the room and the patients placed unconscious. In one group actual corrective surgery took place. In the second group no beneficial surgery was conducted and only fluid was removed from the area. After the operation both groups recovered from the illness in the very same manner. The group that had not received any corrective surgery recovered equally as well as the group that had the actual surgery performed.

In other cases patients were given tablets and told of the effects that they would have on them. In this case the patients were told the opposite of the actual effects of the tablets. The strange thing is that they experienced the effects that were suggested to them and not the ones that are normally experienced as a result of ingestion. In each case the patients experienced that which they *expected* to experience and *believed* they would. They had no reason to think otherwise and therefore had no conflicting thought to hinder the object of their belief.

It's All In Your Mind

A thought with desire and belief will manifest in reality in the absence of any conflicting thoughts.

You must think positive and hold only the positive image outcome in your mind in order to conduct the energy by the nature of your thoughts. Any negative thoughts cut off the flow of the power and sabotage the result. Decide to make thinking positive a part of your daily habits.

Expectancy!

If you are to truly discover the magic in your mind, you must *expect* the object of your desire to happen. It is possible that you may desire a thing strongly; you may even believe that it is possible, but it is another thing to expect it to happen. To truly expect that something will happen is to demonstrate the principle of faith on a whole new level. In order to manifest miracles in your life, you must *expect* miracles to happen in your life. In order to meet your ideal partner you must *expect* to meet your ideal partner. Cultivate the principle of positive expectancy in the garden of your mind. Some might say, that you are setting yourself up for disappointment if you expect things to happen. This is counter to any great achievement made by man. The bible states, "Anything is possible to he that believeth." This is not just the fanciful rambling of a dreamer it is divine truth. In order to step up the vibration of your thought, you should emotionalise your thought with a high level of expectation that the object of your desire is not only possible, but will happen or even better, has already happened in the eternal now. By so doing you shall be taking giant leaps towards your higher potential. How do I develop expectancy you may ask? The answer is quit simple, you visualise clearly the image of that which you desire in your mind. Think of it as clearly as you can manage, then affirm that it is so, and that divine intelligence is bringing this thing into your life. It is best to include all the senses when you imagine the thing happening. If you want that brand new car, imagine yourself in it, take a look around the cabin, smell the new leather interior, hear in you mind the hum of the engine and the traction of the wheels on the ground, imagine the soft feel of the leather seats against your skin. The more detail the better. Revel in your visualisation and include your positive information that you already own the car, and include a positive emotion such as

"I am happily driving my own new silver Mercedes Benz E320"

The more specific you are the more accurately you shall manifest the object in your life. The next step is also important in cultivating the emotion of keyed up expectancy, and that is to adopt the physiology or posture that you normally do when you are successful. Say to yourself in the same voice and tone you do when something great and of significance has been achieved by you. A good example is to note the way you celebrate a goal of your favourite sports team. Do you arch a triumphant fist through the air and say, "Yes!?" Well use this as a trigger to program your goal before it happens" Now we have an even more effective tool for keying up our level of expectancy.

"Yes! (Arched fist through the air) I am happily driving my own new silver Mercedes E320 now!"

Repetition is the key! Once you repeat the above with enough emotion and focus on your desire, it will sink into the deeper levels of your mind. An even more beneficial state for impregnating the mind with such positive statements shall be discussed in a later section.

4. Be Persistent Towards Attaining It and Learn From Your Outcomes.

Persistence!

Sometimes nature will test you and the odds against you will seem insurmountable, however if you will keep going and not give up, you will eventually succeed. It is as if she wants to verify if you are worthy and the way to prove your worthiness is to persist in your endeavour. The one who succeeds is the one who believes he can and keeps on going until he succeeds no matter what is thrown their way. In order to see examples of this all you need to do is read the Biography of top performers in any area. If you read about the most successful business and sports personalities, you will find that they overcame huge obstacles and competition to reach the top. You must take on an attitude of persistence and never give up until you succeed. This is absolutely vital and you must keep on keeping on if you are to reach your goal. The path to success can be a winding and rocky one, and it takes faith and persistence to reach the end. You may recall an old movie called the Wizard of Oz, and in it a young girl, Dorothy had set out to find the Emerald city. A wicked witch of the North had done all in her power to stop her, however Dorothy and her team of friends succeeded in reaching the Emerald city in spite of the odds stacked against them. Of coarse the movie was simple fiction, but it offers a very good example of the principles of success and the path of life. Like all timeless classics it contains great elements of truth in it. Along with the fact that everyone has within them all the brains, heart and courage to do anything that they desire to do. So follow the yellow brick road to your destiny and don't give up until you get there.

One of the main characteristics of successful people is unwavering persistence. Persistence is the quality you must develop and it is closely allied with faith and belief. You must believe whole heartedly in what you are doing and have the faith to continue until it is realized. You must keep on trying until you succeed at what you are going to accomplish. One of the greatest examples of persistence was Thomas Edison, the inventor of the light bulb. He had tried over ten thousand times to create the light bulb. When asked why he continued to go on when he had failed so many times, he simply stated that he had not failed, but he had learned ten thousand things that do not work and was therefore ten thousand steps closer to solving the problem. And sure enough he did succeed. You only have to look around you and see the benefits of the determination of this great mind.

Learn from your outcomes.

Don't be like a fly banging constantly against a pane of glass, getting nowhere as it keeps on ramming itself into the window. Learn from the results that you produce and change until you achieve your desired outcome. In order to overcome your fear of failure you must understand that life's greatest lessons come from our failures. Realize that failure is not actually a failure, but rather it is a valuable lesson in what doesn't work. So what I want you to do is instead of using the word failure use the word FEEDBACK. Instead of beating yourself up over things that you might not have accomplished, say to yourself that this is valuable feedback and quickly follow with the question, what valuable lesson have I learned from this? Where is the opportunity in this? This will soon begin to change how you view your actions. It will empower you to try more and not to be immobilized by temporary setbacks. Of coarse this seems easier said than done, but if you let this become a habitual response to events, you will find that instead of getting frustrated and giving up, you begin to see the value in the FEEDBACK. Even losses in sport, a relationship that didn't quite work or failing a test, all have something to teach you if you seek to act on them and improve on the FEEDBACK they offer. This requires a shift in your attitude. The important thing is then to make adjustments and change based on the negative feedback that you have received. Keep altering your coarse until you reach your destination. Do not be stopped by obstacles, go around them and if you have to go through them.

5. Be Willing To Pay The Price For Its Attainment.

You must be ready to accept success.

If you manage to woo success to you, you must be ready for it and all that goes with it. There is little point in saying that you want to be famous if you are not prepared to sit in front of a camera and conduct interviews on TV or perform in front of an audience. Very often you may go through all the other steps only to sabotage yourself at the last hurtle by not actually being truly ready or prepared for a thing. So you need to be able to welcome all that comes with the thing that you ask. This is vital and a lack of understanding of this principle can bewilder people as to why they had not reached their dream. Apart from being ready to accept a thing you will have to put up with many long hours and be prepared to do whatever it takes to reach your goal. Thus the prospective doctor must put in many years of study and internship, before arriving at the career that he or she imagine themselves to be doing. Many desire to be a track star or to win the Olympics, but are not prepared to pay the price of attaining such a status.

It's All In Your Mind

The people that do succeed are those that are prepared to pay the price of weeks, months, years of hard training and discipline. Even change of diet and conditioning and all without any guarantee of success except in the faith they have in themselves. In order to achieve extraordinary results one must be prepared to make an extraordinary effort, with the odd exception of those that have incredible natural talent. Even they must work hard at perfecting their talent. The singer must be prepared to do the tedious touring of smaller venues on the road to the big stadiums. What helps people to pay the price is to have a big enough desire, to like that which they do, and to have an unshakable faith that they will absolutely achieve that which they are setting out to achieve. With such a combination humans have surpassed all kinds of barriers and achieved wonderful things. It's a simple rule of success, and you must be prepared to pay the price if you are to attain your dreams. If not, then success shall always be just beyond your reach. So woo her and prove to her that you are worthy and begin now to demonstrate that you are prepared to do what it takes.

It's All In Your Mind

Be, Do and Have Your Way to Happiness and Success!

The combination that unlocks your life of riches is Be, Do, Have. Let me explain what is meant by each of these, and the significance of the arrangement of these words. Most people think that they must *have* something, in order to *do* the things they like, and then they can *be* happier. Like certain other mind principles, this is in fact the mirror opposite of the correct syntax for to reach the stage of being happy. It is one of the most widely misunderstood routes to genuine contentment and happiness. Before going into that aspect, let's examine briefly the idea that most people have of how to get on in life. Let's say that you are seeking the coveted management promotion in work. You may think if only I will have that job, I will be able to do the things that other managers do and afford the lifestyle that managers can, and then I'll be happy. The first thing to note here is that there is a condition placed on being happy. There is a stage that must be reached in order to be happy. Please understand that this is self inflicted and will always keep you one step away from happiness. That is why so many so-called successful people are disillusioned by their lack of happiness. They always believe that it will come after the *having* stage, and then when they have the thing they realize that it was not accompanied by the happiness aspect they expected. Stop and think about that for a moment and take the time to apply it to your own approach to happiness and to realize how you are actually remaining one step away by doing this. That is why so many of the famous people with all the riches and fame are still talking about being so unhappy and then turn to drugs and alcohol in a desperate bid to feel the happiness that keeps alluding them.

It's All In Your Mind

Understand that you can decide to be happy now, in this very moment. Not when you have the next Mercedes, or the bigger home or the new bathroom, the ideal husband or wife. You can be happy right now, no matter what your circumstance may be. *It is a matter of shifting your perception to the NOW and realizing that happiness comes from within.* Did you ever notice how you interact with the world when you feel euphoric or on certain happy occasions? You deal with people in a certain way and they respond in kind, you feel like you can take on the world and even the sunshine seems more beautiful. Recall those times; focus on it for as long as you can. Study those that appear to be happy and try to gain an understanding as to why they are so. You will find that the answer is quite simple in those that are consistently happy. You may even be irritated to find that they simply decided to be happy. They realized that they had the power to focus on certain aspects of life in the NOW and that it worked for them. They are *keeping their mind on the things that make them happy.* Think about it for a moment. Why is it that many executives with all the wealth go around with such a degree of unhappiness, when the person that cleans the toilet's in the office seems so happy and content. How could that be? It's the way they use their brains, that's why. *Again it's a matter of deciding what to focus on in each moment of your life.* Decide now to focus on the things that make you happy. We all have things that we are or should be thankful for. The air in your lungs, family friends or most importantly our relationship to God. Lift the fog, drop the weight from your shoulders for a moment and change the things you focus on. Stop trying to juggle the myriad of circumstances and images of failure and deprivation that are out there. Ask yourself the question. *What can I be happy about NOW?*

It's All In Your Mind

Jesus said, "Ask and I will answer, seek and you will find, knock and the door shall be opened to you" Well that's great advice as far as I'm concerned. First ask the question of God, and your own mind, "What can I be happy about now?" Your mind will start to change focus as it assimilates this question. It will provide the answer. You may find it in the simple things, in the affection of a loyal pet, in a flower, in a loved one, or in a simple personal relationship with God. Seek and you will find. Now back to the promotion example. The truth is that in order to quicker manifest the likelihood of getting that position you must first *be* like a manager. You must act the part. Act the part of a manager and do the kinds of things that a manager does and you will soon find that you will have that job. Mainly because you will have demonstrated the kinds of traits that are desirable for such a position. I'm not saying go around like you own the place and are already the manager. No that would draw the opposite response. What I am saying is that you should *be* and act with all the qualities of a good manager, do the kinds of things that demonstrate your ability to perform such tasks, take on the responsibilities that may be on offer, show leadership qualities and do everything as well as you possibly can. Make it your own operating principles to do things in the spirit of excellence, and I guarantee you that you will magnetise yourself to the kinds of positions that you would like. Others will have taken note of how you are management material. Instead what many do is go about demonstrating no initiative and then complain bitterly when they feel they have been passed over. Until you can shine the light on yourself and truthfully assess how your behaviours and attitudes are effecting the way you experience the world. When making decisions ask yourself "How would a competent manager do this?" Even better still, pick somebody that you admire in such a position and model his or her behaviour as closely as possible. See yourself doing things as well if not better than them and elect to implement that in your behaviour. So it is as applicable in the work place as it is to simple happiness.

So to recap, you should decide to *be* happy now, and by being you shall *do* the correct things, and then you will *have* all the things you need. Study the order of these things, and they will open the combination of the lock that has been holding you back so far.

It's All In Your Mind

Use Your Subconscious Intuition to Solve Problems.

Place more trust in your intuition. It shall work more effectively when you trust in it and gain its cooperation. Begin to give it more tasks and then release them in faith to your higher self. You may need the answer to a particular problem or question that you have. An effective way to get a response is to turn it over to your powerful subconscious mind, by stating "Answer this for me God" or "Attend to this for me God" Then positively expect the answer. It may not come immediately, but at a later stage when your mind is busy with other things. It may come to you as a sudden flash and usually complete and accompanied by a feeling of excitement. Trust in the answer or jot it down the moment you receive it. Always have a pen and paper at the ready.

The four steps for solving problems with your creative mind are as follows.

1. Specify the problem clearly. Define it.
2. Concentrate hard, research and do all you can to solve the problem with your normal conscious mind.
3. If you still did not find the answer by conscious thinking, turn it over to your subconscious mind to provide the answer for you. "Attend to this for me"
4. Give thanks for the answer.

Then simply relax and go about other tasks with the expectancy that you will receive the answer to that which you ask. Your mind shall return the answer at possibly an unexpected time. You may try to give a time limit or set a specific time when you expect to get the answer, however more often than not the answer will come at a time when you do not expect it. A good receptive state is to remain in a kind of relaxed alertness.

It's All In Your Mind

The 10 Steps of Scientific Prayer

So I tell you, whatever you ask for in prayer, believe that you have received it, and it will be yours.

Mark 11:24

1. Take four deep breaths in through the nose and exhale quickly out through the mouth. Relax your mind and body.

2. Visualise a shaft of white light filled with loving energy and the Holy Spirit passing through the top of your head and channelling through your entire body and radiating all about you.

3. Affirm the statement, "The Universal Life Force is flowing through me now" with feeling and a sense of excitement.

4. Affirm that you channel your higher self for the purpose of communicating your desired goal or result.

5. Request that your higher self and all knowing subconscious guide and direct you to your higher purpose and also add a specific request.

6. Visualise with emotion, feeling, and a sense of expectancy that your desired outcome is already achieved.

7. Thank your higher self for its help and lovingly request that it also communicate your desire to the infinite intelligence, infinite well of love and almighty creator (GOD). State that you offer the mana, or life force that you gather in the preceding four breaths as an offering to create that which you ask. (You may also take another 4 deep breaths and draw more life force through you for this purpose.) Be as joyful and happy as you can possibly manage when expressing your appreciation. Animate your features, draw in your breath and clench your fists, smile and raise your head and with a great sense of

excitement and express your appreciation with all your might. The more you express your appreciation the closer you will become to the great Almighty that is everywhere and always.

8. Affirm "I believe, I believe, I believe. I am grateful and give thanks that it is so.

9. Do something physical to demonstrate your faith that your request shall be fulfilled. If you desired a car, then buy something, even small for it as a demonstration to your higher self that you actually expect the fulfilment of your desire. Leave it in faith to your higher faculties and understand that it will manifest in your reality. Have patience, and don't dig up the seeds that you have sown. Allow them time to blossom.

10. Repeat with feeling three times daily. Once in the morning, once in the evening and once at night before retiring to bed.

Section 3

Relaxation and The Mind Studio Method

"It is in moments of stillness that we become one with the universe and ourselves."

Up until now you have gained an understanding that there are different levels to your mind and that that your subconscious mind is capable of creating and influencing all the conditions in your life. Let us now examine how to open the channels of communication with your subconscious mind and to give it some tools for communicating directly with you. I understand that these concepts and techniques may appear a little strange to you and I ask that you do not underestimate their effectiveness. I have tried and used them in my own life and have been amazed at the changes that it can bring about. It is very important to learn how to relax and to have moments of stillness and quietude to yourself on a daily basis. Relaxation is very good for you and has physiological, mental and spiritual benefits to it.

Let us first examine the effects of stress on your body and why it is important to learn to relax. There is no doubt that we live in an age when stress is a major problem in society. Stress related illness is costing companies and economies billions of dollars each year and still people are not provided with adequate tools or techniques to deal with the effects of stress. Many factors can bring it on, an ever increasing and never ending workload, an unreasonable or demanding manager, financial pressures, problems in the home etc. The causes are many and varied and the effects can be both mental and physical. Physical effects can include a racing heart, shallow rapid breathing, tense muscles, increased blood pressure, trembling and shivering. If sustained may result in nervous exhaustion and lethargy. This can further be exacerbated by the onset of stress related insomnia.

The cognitive effects can be a lack of ability to concentrate and remember things.

Longer term stress may bring on panic attacks, social anxiety neurosis, depression and obsessive compulsive disorders and substance abuse to mention but a few. Clearly it is important for society and the sufferers of this condition to know how to identify it and deal with it before it develops into more severe symptoms. Your body is designed to give you both positive and negative feedback in the form of pain and pleasure. It is nature's way of communicating with you. Remember we said that the mind cannot tell the difference between an imagined scenario and one that is actually happening. This can be both beneficial and damaging depending on how aware you are of the link. One of the best ways to become aware of the communication is to pay attention to what your body tells you. The body communicates with you intelligently all the time, and you ignore it at your peril. It operates on the principle of cause and effect. When you endure a prolonged stressful situation your body will communicate with you along the way. It will be in the form of tenseness, a racing heart and some of the above symptoms. This is your subconscious mind saying, this behaviour needs to stop or change in order to bring to your attention the effect this is having on you. It is very like the oil temperature warning light in a car when the oil is too low. A lot of people ignore these signals. The subconscious mind notes that the behaviour has not changed to a satisfactory degree and sends another warning this time more potent. In this case the person may feel a sudden onset of panic, a deep and gnawing sense of anxiety and fear. If the person chooses to ignore this and continue to place themselves in the stressful situation and behave in a certain way. The subconscious mind, will say, "Ok I've sent you several warnings and you have not listened. What you are doing is very damaging to your system, so I will have to shut you down for a while."

Then what happens is the person simply has a system breakdown and may be so nervously exhausted that they physically cannot get out of bed or face another person. I don't like the term, but it has been called a nervous breakdown. Unfortunately, the ego part of the personality that urged you to deny anything was wrong now does not want you in any way to admit to anyone else that it has happened and may try to stop you from seeking the necessary help. In order to protect itself the ego may prevent you from entering any situation that may bring on the panic and damage the self-esteem.

At a physiological level what has been happening is that your mind has been reacting to your fears as if they were a real threat to your safety. It is a reaction built into your brain's survival mechanism. Psychologists call it the fight or flight mechanism. Basically, it prepares your body to fight a threatening foe or to flee the situation in time to save yourself. It is an automatic trigger system that reacts to stressful situations. It serves man well in certain situations such as if you step out in front of a car and only hear the horn at the last second. Your adrenalin gland shoots adrenalin into your bloodstream, which raises your blood pressure, quickens your heart and provides the energy to the muscles to do what is necessary, and so your body jumps in a split second and you are saved. It is for such circumstances that the mechanism has been designed. However, the same reaction occurs in the body when you imagine or experience a stressful situation. The adrenalin is released into the body in like manner and your body prepares for fight or flight. The heart quickens, the muscles tremble with energy and it is not dissipated because there is no physical action taking place to dissipate this excess energy that is building up in the body. It may be likened to placing your foot on the accelerator and the brake in a car at the same time. What happens is that the body of the car shudders in much the same way that your body shudders or trembles. If the powerful subconscious detects that there is too much adrenalin in the body it releases a "stress hormone" called cortisone. This counteracts the effects of the adrenalin and begins to stabilise the body. The thing is that the more stress we experience, the more adrenalin is used and then more cortisone is released to deal with it. Over an extended period we begin to deplete our resources of this hormone and it is then drawn from other important functions in the body and has a harmful knock on effect.

Relax and Breathe Your Way To Maximum Well-being.

There is a wonderful substance that you can use to bring yourself to optimum health, relaxation, and increase your mental performance. What is it? Oxygen of coarse. Techniques in rhythmic breathing are extremely effective in improving your health and improving your mental operating faculties. It figures since your brain uses up to 25% of your entire oxygen intake and uses up to 20% of your body's energy. It is clear that your brain needs a good oxygen supply to perform at optimum levels. It is vital to feeling good and energetic, and there are effective common sense ways of making better use of this fabulous resource. With rhythmic breathing techniques you increase the oxygen levels reaching your brain and foster better blood flow. The brain uses oxygen to burn its fuel, glucose, and by increasing the flow to your brain you're helping it to operate more efficiently. One of the easiest ways to ensure a good oxygen intake is to get out for a walk in the fresh air. Best to avoid the bustling traffic and all that carbon dioxide wouldn't you say. Every city's planning authorities have set aside parkland and greens where the folks can walk around at their leisure. Your lymphatic system will benefit from the exercise as well as the fresh air. I especially love to walk along by the ocean. It is refreshing no matter what the time of year. The area near the impact zone of the waves, where they roll and swash ashore is packed with ionised air that is beneficial to your health. Water pummelled or rushing through the air at a fast pace causes the negative ionisation of the air particles, and this ionised air is very easily carried in the blood stream and processed in the brain more efficiently. This brings about a sense of well-being. Add to the mix the relaxing sound of the swashing waves and the nice scenery and you have the best health recipe you could ask for.

I can't encourage people enough to get out into the fresh air and sunshine and to go for a walk. Another great exercise that ensures a good overall workout and oxygenation of the body is swimming. If you don't know how learn if not just for your health then for safety reasons. At least take a moment to synthesise how your lifestyle might be contributing to ill health. Ask yourself and look at your daily activities and see how they are cheating you from proper health. Do you drink multiple cups of coffee a day and smoke heavily? Do you sit still at a computer terminal from morning to night and then go to the pub and sit still in a smoky atmosphere after work or veg out in from of the television for the rest of the night. This is more or less what I would call passive living. Start becoming more active in your choices. If you can't afford to join a gym, then simply take frequent walks.

Here is an effective rhythmical breathing exercise that shall help you to relax, and can be done in such a short time as to be useful before stressful situations such as public speaking, meetings or uncomfortable social occasions.

Take a deep breath in through your nose, inhaling for 8 seconds. Then hold your breath for 12 seconds and exhale through your mouth for 10 seconds. Repeat this a number of times and include a favourable affirmation such as "I am confident and calm in all situations" and visualize yourself performing well in the task you are about to undertake.

The reason you should breath in through the nose is that it is designed to filter the air and heat it to a desirable temperature for your lungs.

Another advanced breathing technique used by the Yogi's of the Far East is the Moon Breath. This helps harmonise and balance both sides of the brain so that both hemispheres work in synch with each other.

Place your thumb and forefinger of either hand up to your nostrils. Now block the right nostril with one of your fingers and inhale for a count of 8 through your left nostril. Then hold in your lungs for a count of 12. Then pinch your left nostril and exhale through the right nostril for a count of 10. On the next breath cover your left nostril and breathe in through your right for a count of 8 and so on. Alternate between the nostrils in like fashion approximately 8 to 10 times. This alternates the flow of oxygen between both hemispheres and synchronises them in a harmonious rhythm.

The practice of Rhythmic breathing is vital in the maintaining a good oxygenation of the brain and body.

It's All In Your Mind

Progressive Relaxation.

What we are about to look at now is a way to open up new avenues for you to explore your inner world and reality. You will learn how to relax yourself and then to be able to trigger that relaxed state at times when you need it. You are going to build the tools that will open the channels of communication between you and your all-knowing subconscious mind. It requires that you begin to use the magical properties of your imagination. It is a way of communicating with yourself at a much deeper level and imparting the important changes that you want to see happen in your life. You will be able to have your mind and inner team guide you in many inspiring ways and assist you through your life. I urge you to set aside any apprehension you have and to give it a try. I am only interested in providing you with the most effective and powerful secrets of unlocking the potential of your mind. It is important that you don't feel that you're forcing yourself, enjoy these techniques and they will unlock infinite creativity in you and help you find that inner guidance that will take you along the path to whatever goal you have set yourself.

It's time for some peace and quiet. Find yourself a nice relaxed place where you will be undisturbed. Sit or lie down in a comfortable position. Note it may be beneficial to learn to do this sitting up, as you may be able to reproduce the result while sitting in a waiting room for an interview or a meeting or a live TV show or whatever. You are now going to progressively relax yourself, and your aim is to reach a level of Alpha relaxation. You operate at different brain wavelengths during the day. They are placed into four characteristic ranges, Beta, Alpha, Theta, and Delta. Each is characterised by a set frequency or rhythm called (brain wave) cycles per second. Their range is as follows, Beta brain waves are between 13-30 cycles per second and represent when you are in a fully awake alert and active state. Alpha brain waves are between 8 to 12 cycles per second, and are present when you are in a relaxed dreamy state, Theta waves are between 4 to 8 cycles per second and are characteristic of when you are in a deep meditative state. Finally, Delta brain waves are produced when you are in a deep sleep and are between 0.5 and 4 cycles per second.

Our goal is to reach the Alpha state of relaxation. It is at this level that you may communicate instructions and images directly to your powerful subconscious mind in a more effective way. Now that you have found a comfortable position and are relaxed. You should close your eyes, and turn them up approximately 45 degrees inside the eyelid. This shall enhance your Alpha state and improve your receptivity to your own positive messages and start to harmonise the communication between your left and right brain hemispheres. It shall place the left logical functions to the rear and the right imaginative faculties to the fore.

Count from 50 to 1 while concentrating on relaxing each part of your body from head to toe. Take a deep breath in through your nose, inhaling for 8 seconds. Hold for 12 and then release for 10 seconds. Start with the tips of your hair and imagine a warm golden energy descending on the tips of your hair and running down to the roots of your hair. Feel yourself relax. Count from 50 to 40, when you reach forty imagine the golden ray of relaxing warmth descend through your facial muscles relaxing your eyes and mouth as it descends to your neck. Focus your attention on each part of the body as the light descends through you and feel yourself relax. Keeping your breathing deep and slow, breathing in and out of your nose. Count from 40-30 and imagine your neck becoming relaxed and comfortable as the ray of light passes through every cell and relaxes it. Focus your attention on your shoulders and right arm, elbow wrist, hand and fingers. Then the same for the left arm. As you reach 30 say to yourself that you are feeling calm relaxed and comfortable. Count from 29-20 and concentrate on the relaxation of each muscle group down your chest and abdomen. When you reach the count of 20 say to yourself, I am feeling calm and relaxed. Then count from 19-10, concentrating your attention on each leg separately. Feeling the thighs relax and become heavy, all the time imagining this golden glow of light descending your body. At the count of ten say to yourself "I am calm and relaxed" Continue your count from 9-5 and you shall imagine that your knees, calves, shins, feet and toes are relaxed. Concentrate on each muscle and let it relax. At the count of five you shall say to yourself that when you reach the count of 1 you shall be fully relaxed and calm. Then count from 4-0. Take a slow deep breath in and exhale. At this point you will feel completely relaxed and at ease. Your entire body will be relaxed and all tension should be released from your system. Well done if you feel relaxed and tranquil then you have reached the Alpha state successfully.

It is at this level that you may begin to use positive affirmations and creative visualisation to impress on your subconscious mind the things that you want.

It's All In Your Mind

Soon we will integrate this level with specific mind tools and visualizations that shall improve your intuition and assist in the manifestation of your dreams.

After you have spent a few moments imagining that which you would like to be and have in your life in as clear and detailed a fashion as you can manage. Let's take you back to your fully awake state again.

Begin to count from 1-5 and say to yourself when I reach the count of 5 I will be wide-awake, happy and healthy. Proceed to count, and upon reaching 5 say to yourself "I am wide awake, feeling more healthy and happy."

Then open your eyes and go about your day. For some this will come as a great rest period and a welcome break in an otherwise hectic day. The majority will agree that it is a pleasant and enjoyable experience.

Once you learn how to reach these levels of relaxation and Alpha state you can go on to perform wonderful tasks. You will begin to counteract and reduce the effects of stress, gain insights and even heal yourself.

Inducing Alpha and balance between your brain's hemispheres can be achieved through the medium of music.

The Universe and everything in it is in a constant state of vibration. Even our own planet has its own rhythm and beat within existence. Music affects us in many ways, and to a degree that some of us would care not to know.

It's All In Your Mind

Extensive studies in the area of accelerative learning have revealed the beneficial effects that certain types of music have on our minds. Certain types of classical music have been shown to produce Alpha state rhythms in our brains and balance the left and right hemispheres. The result being an enhanced learning ability and a significant improvement in memory. If you relax your muscles, breath deeply and close your eyes, you have a good chance of quickly entering the Alpha state. Our mental capacity increases when we can utilise both hemispheres to a greater degree for a given task. Even plants have been noted to grow more abundantly when bathed in certain types of Baroque garden music. It is interesting to note that many creative minds and great mathematicians engaged in activities that stimulated both hemispheres of the brain. Einstein was not only a great mathematician, but also a concert level violinist too. I was interested to read that Paul Gauguin would always have the music of Puccini playing away in the background as he painted. Other great mathematicians were also noted to be talented jugglers. Juggling being a fun activity is extremely effective in balancing the hemispheres while at the same time helping to entertain others too, not to mention earning pocket money if you're really good. The specific music that I listen to for the beneficial effects that I've been talking about has been Baroque garden and Music by Vivaldi, Mozart, Beethoven, and Bach. In their wonderful book entitled, Superlearning 2000, Sheila Ostrander and Lynn Schroeder point out that baroque garden is paced at 60 beats per minute and this synchronises our brain waves harmoniously in balance. I've tried a number of the classical music and Baroque garden music and I recommend the Four Seasons by Vivaldi, and Air in G by J S Bach, The Magic Flute by Mozart. I've found these particularly helpful in assisting me to concentrate and I'm listening to these as these letters hit the page.

We have all heard certain songs that conjure up moods of an inspiring nature. They may remind you of a good time or a place where you first heard that particular song. Others can make you feel down by their sombre tones and rhythms, and others still can make you feel aggressive and violent. There is little doubt that music affects us emotionally and it is important to consciously decide what kind you choose to listen to. The native tribes of the world have all used music in their cultures and rituals. The synchronous droning of the African tribes helps them harmonise as one mind. They sing, dance and move as one. So use the magic of music for your benefit. Make yourself a tape of the specific songs that conjure up good memories for you, and on occasions when you could do with a pick me up, play it. If you want to improve your recall of texts you read while studying, play sixty beat per minute Baroque garden music in the background to aid your concentration and memory. Pay attention to the influence that certain kinds of music have on your moods and then choose the ones that best suit your needs.

It's All In Your Mind

Your Personal Mind Counsellors and the Mind Studio.

What you are about to do now requires the work of your imagination and is a secret method used by many of the worlds richest and most successful men. Napoleon Hill introduced this concept in his outstanding book, Think and Grow Rich and called it the mastermind alliance. Through it you may seem to come by information in your mind that you would not otherwise have access to. You are going to create a Mind Studio and team of counsellors in your mind. By doing so you will open up new channels for your creative subconscious to communicate ideas and thoughts to you that will astound you. The method requires repetition, persistence and practice, but if you will work at it and trust in it, you will be rewarded for the rest of your life. What you are first going to do is choose a group of people whom you admire and would choose to seek their counsel on matters of life and success. It doesn't matter whether they are alive or passed on. You should choose a group that have represented the best of all qualities in the areas relating to life and your set of goals. If you want to start a business, choose someone whom you consider being an all time great in the field. You may choose artists and philosophers to give you guidance. If you want to be a writer you may want to choose your favourite author. If you want to make it in sport choose your hero. You should choose up to 12 people as your mind counsellors. You may decide to choose greats such as Einstein, Leonardo De Vinci, and Abraham Lincoln.

Now keep the group in mind. Let them sit around a conference table and imagine them as if they were real in your mind. Imagine how they interact with each other and you will introduce yourself to each of them in turn and begin a mental relationship with them. As clear as you can you should imagine how they act and speak. In order to aid you in this you should learn as much about them as possible, read their biographies and become familiar with their philosophies and methods. Remember it doesn't have to be anyone famous it could well be a teacher or local priest or businessman that you admire for a specific quality that you would like instilled in you and your character. It can be anything from humour, confidence, courage, passion and whatever desirable qualities you would like.

When you mentally introduce yourself to them you should imagine that you are talking to them as if they are real. In a sense, at the electromagnetic and neuro-transmitter level they are. If you have a particular question or problem that you need to solve you can conduct the above relaxation exercise and then seek counsel from them. For example you may ask, "How would Abraham Lincoln act in this situation? What would he say and do?" Then sit at the conference table and ask him yourself, "Abraham Lincoln this is the situation…(outline it)…what would you do and say to solve this problem? Instil in my mind and character your wisdom and poise to solve this problem. Then imagine what he will answer. Do not try to force it, release your imagination and allow it to answer by not judging the first response or trying to analyse it. You will find that they can take on a life of their own. Sometimes they will not answer immediately but at a later time.

If you persist it will work. I'm not suggesting that you make hasty decisions and blame the group in your head, then those around you would think you are mad. What you should do is use this as a way of developing your intuition. Help your mind help you.

Next you are going to produce the Mind Studio in which you direct and produce the movie of your life.

It's All In Your Mind

The Mind Studio.

Conduct the relaxation exercise outlined above, and when you reach your Alpha level begin to construct your Mind Studio for directing, broadcasting, and receiving the life of your dreams.

Imagine that you are coming across a closed door and it is much like the closed door at a movie theatre. On the door is written "I am I" and you make your way in. As you enter you notice that the atmosphere is relaxed, calm and welcoming. You close the door behind you and take a look around. In the centre of the room is a chair much like that of a movie director, and on the back it has your name written on it. Imagine that this chair is the chair of the director, the seat of the WILL. You stroll forward and sit yourself down comfortably in the chair. At the front of the studio is a large screen, which is about six feet in front of your chair. The screen is as large as you like. In front of you is a control panel with various dials and switches and a computer keyboard built into the control panel. You glance over the panel and note that it has an aerial sticking up. This shall be used to send and receive thoughts for the purposes of the communication of ideas. There is also a double deck Mini-Disc/DVD player and recorder on the panel. One of the double decks is for playing and the other for recording. To your left is a conference table with microphones on it and your mastermind group are seated there. They greet you and welcome you to the mind studio, they are smiling and happy that you have arrived. You look around the room and note that there are surround speakers all around the room. You also notice that above there is a green light above the screen, which states *ON AIR* much like those at a TV or radio broadcasting station. The studio is ultra-high-tech with the latest equipment. In front of you is a microphone, and beside it is a switch for when you talk. Go ahead and toggle the switch and speak into the microphone. Imagine that you hear your voice come through all the surround speakers crisp and clear. Beside that switch is a button in the red off position and you switch it to the green position, and when you do the *ON AIR* light illuminates beside the screen and the screen comes on. First of all, a screen saver appears. It starts off as a red dot in the centre of the screen, which increases in size until the entire screen is red and the red illuminates the room. The same thing happens with the next colour, which is orange, the dot starts in the centre and fills the entire screen and then another dot appears in the centre this time it is yellow. Then a green dot appears and expands, then a blue one and then an indigo until finally violet fills the screen and it turns white again.

At this point you notice that the screen has settled on a screen containing various icons such as those on a computer and a flashing cursor on the screen. You notice that one is an icon for email, another for memories and another for TV channels.

Now you take a quick look around the rest of the room and note that the projector illuminating the screen is coming from a booth up in the rear, which is a light source, you intuitively know that this is your higher creative self.

To the right hand side is a group of teleporters like those in Star Trek. These are used to materialize things and people and also to transport you to any location you wish at the flash of a thought. Towards the rear are a stretcher style bed and a medicine cabinet. You step over and have a quick glance in the medicine cabinet and you notice that there are capsules for healing all kinds of ailments. One of the packs you pick up has confidence labelled on the front, and one to be taken daily. You pop the cap open and take one of these imaginary pills, and feel it descend into your stomach. You close the cabinet and head back to the chair.

You have now established your Mind Studio, and you may visit it for ideas and healing anytime that you desire.

Count yourself out again from one to five and again affirming that you will be wide-awake and feeling healthy and happy.

You now have at your disposal the most effective tools you could ask for to communicate with the all-knowing world within. It is a multimedia studio able to communicate with others at a subconscious level and to receive ideas for inventions, writing songs, directing future scenes in your life, as you would like to have them materialize. The only limits to the applications of your Mind Studio are the limits of your imagination. If you find it hard to visualize each of them, don't worry it will come with practice. A tip to help you visualize is as follows, close your eyes and imagine that you are entering a scene that you are very familiar to you. Let's use your bedroom as an example. Imagine your bed, the wardrobes, the layout, as much details as you can. Take a walk around it and imagine you are actually there. Add to the experience by imagining that you are touching some of the objects there. This will help you practice the art of imagining and visualising.

It's All In Your Mind

Receiving Answers and Feedback in the Mind Studio.

Once again do your progressive relaxation exercise and count yourself down
to your 0 level and Alpha state. Enter your Mind Studio and toggle the
switch to ON AIR and see the colour sequence screen saver go through the
motions until it settles on violet and back to white. Greet your mind
counsellors also. Take a moment to imagine a conversation with them. It is
always a good idea to do this as the answer to a question you may have
asked in a previous visit to your Mind Studio. Your powerful subconscious
may have come up with the answer in the meantime and will communicate it
to you through the channel of the most appropriate member of your advisory
team. If this occurs it will happen automatically and in your mind you will
receive the answer. One of the benefits of the Mind Studio is that it provides
your inner self a very effective channel for communicating with you. You
may click on the inbox of your screen email and check for any message that
may have arrived. Switch the screen to TV mode and watch the images that
may be streaming across the screen. If you are a person that tends to receive
messages by an inner voice in your head, then turn on your Mind Studio
radio receiving set, and also check your mind message minder. This may
induce your mind to release the message to you at that moment. Don't
worry if each of these options does not offer a satisfactory response in you at
the start. Persist and your mind will realize that you are committed to this
two-way communication process and will begin to work with you in a
clearer way. Once you receive the message acknowledge it with thanks and
then decide to remember such feedback and to use it. You should make use
of the information that you receive within a short or appropriate amount of
time. Your mind will give you intuitions and advice, but if you choose to

ignore this information and do something to the contrary then you will have broken one of the unwritten laws of communicating with your inner self. If you do not pay some heed to the messages that you receive then your subconscious will close that channel of communication for a time until you prove otherwise. It is too powerful and conducting too many important tasks to be wasting time sending messages that are ignored.

This is a multimedia Mind Studio and you may even receive extra-sensory feedback by olfactory or scent or even feeling. Simply imagine an air conditioner unit along the bottom of the screen and this shall pump scents into the room of what images are on the screen. So if you imagine a wonderful scene on the screen of Tahiti for example, you may notice the scent of vanilla plants being pumped into the Mind Studio. If that is not automatic, imagine the scent in your mind. You may practice this by visualizing a rose on your Mind Studio screen, imagine a bright red rose swaying in a fresh breeze, now imagine that you can now smell the scent coming into the Mind Studio room. If you want to enhance your experience further you may step onto the teleporter and teleport yourself to a field of roses, imagine it in every detail, the colours, the feel and images and temperature. Enjoy the scene before returning to the studio. Bath yourself in your imaginary senses.

Sometimes this can create a physiological response in your body. Remember that your mind cannot tell the difference between a real or clearly imagined thing. So if you imagine that you are sucking on an orange and imagine it clearly you may find yourself salivating. Just as imagined erotic scenes can create a physical reaction in both men and women.

Once you become familiar with how these inner thoughts are affecting literally every aspect of your life, you will begin to take a more active roll in developing yourself and your habits in the right direction.

It's All In Your Mind

Applications of the Mind Studio.

Conduct the progressive relaxation exercise and descend to 0 level. Enter your Mind Studio and sit in the chair at the control panel. Greet your Mind Counsellors and turn on the equipment. Note the screen saver come on with the colour sequence as before. This is an important step and actually assists to change the frequency of your thoughts.

A few of applications may be as follows, and you may think of many other ways to use it.
1. Broadcast a message to your soul mate and call him/her to you.
2. Visualise the ideal day on your screen
3. Program yourself for success in an upcoming task.
b. Switching a bad memory of a task with a new empowering image.
4. Consulting with the Mind Counsellors
5. Conducting self-healing, and healing by prayer for others.
6. Sending Requests
7. Giving Up smoking

You are in the studio and the status is ON AIR, indicating that you are able to broadcast your thought to whomever you want.

It's All In Your Mind

Broadcasting Your Readiness To Meet Your Soul Mate or Ideal Partner.

If you are single you will be able to attract that person to you, and communicate with that person at the subconscious level. In the eternal NOW that message shall reach them and they may respond within a short period of time. It is a form of telepathy. It doesn't matter whether your believe in the process or not the principle will work just as gravity works as an invisible force.

Using the control wheel on the control panel scroll the cursor and click on email on the screen.

In the

To; field on the email, Type: to my ideal soul mate, and copy in the infinite intelligence and infinite well of love.

Then type in the message to them, you may write

"To my soul mate, I love you and welcome you into my life. I am ready to meet you and to enter into a relationship with you on the physical and emotional planes. It shall be a happy and loving relationship and we shall meet each other soon in the correct sequence in time actions and events. The infinite well of love brings us together in divine order, for love is our highest good. My love I call you to me now. Infinite well of love my soul mate shall be ....(Give a brief description of your soul mate...(S)he is loving, caring, sensitive, strong courageous. You may even describe looks if you like, but I don't recommend restricting yourself to looks or hair colours as your subconscious may pick up the signals of the physical person in a public place and pass her by because the hair colour is not right.

Then click send. When you send muster a strong sense of emotion that the thing you have asked for shall be granted. The more emotion you can add to this action the more effective it will be. Repetition with feeling is the key to success in this phase.

The screen then turns to a flying dove with an envelope in its beak and flies into the distance in the screen carrying your message to the recipients.

Alternatively you may switch on the microphone on the control panel and broadcast the message by voice through the aerial and send images via the web cam on your control panel. Feel free to do whichever you feel will be the most effective for you. It is the process of imagination that will work magic in your life. Imagine the mind waves being transmitted through the aerial to the intended recipient, and include as clear a mental image as you can along with the emotionalised words.

After conducting such exercises you may find that so called coincidences may occur and you may find that your automatic mind spots a person out of the blue or directs you to say something to a particular person. In other cases you may decide to attend a social occasion that you would normally avoid, and then meet someone special. In a real sense you will be magnetized to the situation you desire. A word of caution is not to think that just any person is your soul mate. That way you may leave yourself open for disappointment. Use your normal discretion as you would with any stranger and listen to your intuition more closely.

When you do meet the right person, there does tend to be an inner knowing in you that this is the one. For some it is instant and for others it takes a little more time. Have fun and enjoy it. Again it comes down to choice, you can choose not to try and I'm not telling anyone to believe without verifying the results for themselves. Like many of the laws of the science of mind and spirit, believing is seeing.

It's All In Your Mind

Programming Yourself For Success In An Upcoming Event.

Let us use the example that you have to give a talk or sell an idea at an upcoming meeting.

Click the icon on the screen for Life Movie. On the screen shall appear a still of you entering the future scenario. Press record on the DVD recorder on the control panel and note the flashing red record button. Imagine it in as much details as possible the scene you are entering. Visualise the people greeting you and how you act when you sit down. See yourself performing perfectly in the situation. You are confident and handling all inquiries with ease and poise. The people are responding to you in a friendly and smiling way and you know they are in agreement with you. Imagine the scene run through until you reach the successful conclusion and the parting from the meeting. If it is a public speech you might imagine people clapping you and happy that you delivered such a natural and clear speech. Then press stop on the DVD record function.

This is a disassociated movie image in that you saw yourself acting that way on the screen. You may reinforce the effect of this future programming by stepping into the teleporter on the right hand side of the room and imagine yourself being beamed into the future scene. Then proceed to see it unfold as above, but this time through your own eyes as if you were actually there. This is an imagined and associated movie. For some this will seem more real than the disassociated screen exercise.

It's All In Your Mind

If you had a bad experience in the particular activity, such as public speaking in the past you may use a mind control technique to take the take away the disempowering effect of such memories or fears.

Imagine that you call up an unpleasant digital memory DVD of the above that you are not happy with your performance. You do this by simply imagining the scene and the DVD player brings the disc to the record deck.

You can hit the Control and S key on the keyboard and note that the screen splits into two images with a line down the centre of the screen. The one on the right is your fearful memory of how you performed the last time and on the left split screen is a still of the way you would have ideally liked to have performed.

Now you call up the ideal performance movie DVD in the play deck. Remember that the screen is still split and that your ideal scene is on the left and your memorised scene on the right. Now press play on the idea scene DVD and record on the memorised DVD, and note that you are recording over the memory disc, erasing its harmful effects and replacing it with a more empowering scene. The line in the centre begins to move to the right as the ideal movie scene plays out. The other still is being replaced by the scene on the left. It continues until the ideal image is the only one playing on the entire screen and finishes when the scene has played out to its successful conclusion.

It's All In Your Mind

At the deeper levels of mind you are de-fragmenting the impact of bad memories and replacing them with more empowering images.

Creating Your Ideal Day Scene In The Future.

There are two ways you can do this. One is the disassociated scenes which shall be played on your mind screen and the other is the associated scene like the one we dealt with earlier, and it can be achieved in much the same way by imagining teleporting yourself to the actual time and place in the NOW.

I prefer to teleport myself to the actual scene and experience it as if looking through my own eyes. So let's go back to the future! Make sure you have come through all the stages of the relaxation and visualization and reach your Alpha or 0 level.

Step from your life director's chair and step into the teleporter, and imagine you are casting yourself into your ideal future scene. I shall use the example of waking in your dream home with your dream partner. Imagine yourself getting up and walking around your wonderful home. If you want kids or more kids imagine them greeting you in the morning with a loving hug and you notice that they are beaming with energy and are healthy and happy. You stroll to your kitchen and have breakfast and as you plan your day ahead. Do not restrict yourself in your scene. It can be as big or small as you want it. In the world of imagination anything is possible. There could be large fountains in the garden, a beautiful backdrop to an ocean stroll. You may imagine that you are setting off to your ideal job, or if you're are so inclined you may imagine that you're going to contribute at a great charity event that you have organised and are contributing to with your success. You set off in you fabulous car. You're there sitting in the soft leather seats, and can feel the nice grip of the steering wheel. You may continue to imagine your idea day in such fashion until the conclusion.

Then when you return to the teleporter, you should say

"I believe, I believe, I believe"

Then once you have concluded the session, you may count yourself back into a healthy wide-awake state. Often you cannot help but feel good after going through such a scene, after all you have just experienced on one level your ideal day and experienced it in the NOW.

The mind shall begin to work on these images and your powerful subconscious shall work on bringing them into your reality.

It's All In Your Mind

Using the Mind Studio to Help Give Up Smoking.

Enter the studio, go through the relaxation exercise and the screen colour sequence, and greet your Mind Counsellors and your higher self. Take your position at the director's chair and the control panel. On the keyboard imagine yourself hitting Control and S at the same time, and when you do the screen is split in two vertically. On the right hand side is the behaviour you want to change. It may be a picture of you smoking. Connected to this image are a number of smaller images. These images are of the bad effects that this behaviour or habit causes, such as cancer, chesty coughing, yellow teeth, aged skin. Note that they are linked to the image of the smoking.

On the left portion of the screen place an image of the behaviour that you would like to replace it with. It may be eating healthy fruits or doing exercise more often. Now twist the knob marked contrast and sharpness so that the brightness and clarity of this desirable image increases. The undesirable images begin to fade out. Then when it is as clear as you can imagine, hit the switch marked replace program. When you hit this button the image on the left begins to increase in size and take up the full screen. On the other side the images had reduced in size and faded from the screen. This may be done at whatever speed is most effective for you. Some people may wish to feel it move slowly, and others will find it more effective to burst the image across the screen at lightening speed. You may repeat the process a couple of times if you want to reinforce the effect. Breathe deeply, and feel the excitement of what this change will do for you. Know that the change is taking place and affirm the words, "I believe, I believe, I believe."

It's All In Your Mind

You may anchor the sensations with an external stimulus also as a way of reinforcing the new behaviour at a later time. You may play a specific harmonious song in the background and imagine it coming through the speakers of the Mind Studio. Alternatively, you may use a specific scent. At the peak of the excited sensations you produce when visualizing the new behaviour, make use of a certain scent. Place it to your nose and smell the scent as you imagine clearly the image and affirm your belief as above. The scent should be specific. It may be anything from the aroma of coffee, to a particular aftershave or perfume. The idea being that if you feel the urge to conduct the old behaviour, you would pull out the scent and take a whiff, thereby conjuring the clear memory of the images of the new behaviour and causing you to enter that state. The use of scent can be very effective in this purpose and our sense of smell is closely linked to our memory. The mind will not care if it is a real experienced memory or an imagined one. It will draw to the surface either one that is linked effectively to the stimulus or scent.

Next imagine that your Mind Counsellors are clapping and applauding you with smiles and pride. They encourage your successful change. From the disassociated image, you may reinforce the change of habit by stepping into the experience in an associated way through the Mind Studio. Step onto the teleporter and beam yourself into the scene that you imagined on the screen. Imagine as clear as you can manage every detail around you, through your own eyes. Engage the senses as much as possible, the more you do the more you will appeal to the emotions. It is these that fire the neurotransmitters in the brain to form the new pattern as imagined.

It's All In Your Mind

Return to the Mind Studio by simply desiring to be there and imagine yourself there. Count yourself out from 1-5 and affirm that you're wide-awake, healthy and happy.

Changing habits is also greatly assisted by doing something physical that is a substitute for the benefit that you had previously received from the behaviour that you want to change. So to assist your programming, you should also replace the bad habit with something that will bring you an equal or greater benefit and is a more desirable alternative. For example instead of reaching for a cigarette, reach for some healthy food and instead of buying cigarettes buy something else that will be good for you and that you will enjoy more. The pain of giving up a previous habit may be offset by the pleasure of a better alternative.

Final Word

The kingdom of God is within. Look within and you will find more treasures than has ever been discovered in history. It is a greater journey than any Columbus ever undertook. The more people begin to explore the inner universe of the mind, the more we will see abundance, joy and love around us. For enlightened people who discover these truths will never find lack, instead you will find an infinite supply of love, wisdom, and anything that you could ever want or need. You will realize that you are a part of God, and God a part of you. That we are all one! Begin the adventure of a lifetime and explore this inner world of which this book only maps out the shoreline of a vast infinite ocean of truth. Understand that you are a centre point in an infinite ocean of energy called the Universe. You are a spark of the divine and the infinite creator flows, and works through you. I repeat again lest you forget it,

"As within, So Without"

Begin by simply understanding that whatever conditions you want in your life, you can create them. Through awareness you shall start to contemplate the truths that shall resonate within you. Pay attention to your inner sensations, and you will hear the language of the soul. Rejoice for its music shall have fell on receptive ears. Ears that shall hear the music of the flowers and the blast of the sun, and your feet shall tap to the dance of the heavenly music. Discover this, and above all may you realize that It's All In Your Mind! May God Bless you.

Noel Cox

It's All In Your Mind

Recommendations

Develop your own personal library.

One of the best ways to spend your spare moments is to read between the covers of an inspirational book. Read materials that shall enrich your mind and your spirit. When you read, you engage in a conversation with the author and begin to understand the way he or she thinks. There are books out there to teach you any strategy that you may care to learn. Reading expands the mind, and a mind expanded never returns to its original dimensions. What another can do, you can do with the proper training. Seldom will you come across an effective leader in any field who is not an avid reader. Reading acts like a receiving set for telepathy. The words are the frozen thoughts of their authors. When you observe the printed word the circuit is completed and the idea perceived. Certain works will change your life in an instant. The man that started the book is different to the man or woman that shuts the back cover at the other end. Something may resonate a great truth within him or her. An unexplainable gush of excitement and warm energy seems to well up in the individual in whom the higher potential has just been awakened. A surge of truth that has been spoken in the language of the soul. Begin to start your own home library. Invest in it, and if you cannot afford to at this time, then join a local library. Hours spent reading inspirational classics and motivational titles will pay dividends in your life. You may learn to run your own brain and body to a degree that you may never have thought possible. There are strategies on the printed page and on the Internet to train you to do worthwhile things and to reach your higher potential. When you see someone achieve something wonderful, ask yourself how you may achieve even better results. You can lean how to read at speeds many times faster than your current rate. There are strategies for improving your memory to phenomenal degrees, all awaiting your attention and study. Become excited at the knowledge that you can learn that which will allow you do and achieve pretty much anything you want to achieve. Learn all about extraordinary people and how they've achieved the levels of success that you desire for yourself and your family. Read about how Beethoven produced some of the world's greatest masterpieces, even though he himself was deaf. Helen Keller was blind and against all the odds achieved outstanding success and wonderful things in her lifetime. Make more efficient use of your time. Books on tape are a very useful format for to gather information and strategies while commuting to and from work, or college or wherever you may be travelling on a given day. Play them in the background while you conduct your household chores. They shall capture your attention in a relaxed state. Remember what we said about that which we focus on? That's right, it grows in your experience and your life. You become what you think about. When you read and listen to inspirational works, you are focusing on your higher potential and increasing the likelihood of achieving greater success. When I go out for a walk and exercise in the fresh air, I often take an inspirational tape and listen to it on a Walkman, and manage to learn as well as get fitter. Thus your car, your bus, can become a moving library. An hour in traffic becomes an hour in your mobile classroom, and you actually gain from the process. Also by virtue of focus and thought substitution, you shall be focussing more on the positive and less likely to become stressed as you normally would in such circumstances.

Recommended Reading List.

The following is a list of books that I recommend for the student of the science of mind and spirit. They are available at www.magusmind.com

Think and Grow Rich, by Napoleon Hill.

The Power of Your Subconscious Mind, Joseph Murphy Ph D. D. D.

The Secret of the Ages, by Robert Collier.

The Silva Mind Control Method, by Jose Silva and Philip Miele.

Psycho-Cybernetics, by Maxwell Maltz, M.D.,F.I.C.S.

Unlimited Power, by Tony Robbins.

Creative Visualization, by Shakti Gawain.

The Science of Mind, by Ernest Holmes

www.MagusMind.com

Our goal is your Higher Potential

A leading online resource for the products, learning and practice of the science of personal development and helping people reach their higher potential.

If you would like to email the author please feel free to email info@magusmind.com

www.ingramcontent.com/pod-product-compliance
Lightning Source LLC
Chambersburg PA
CBHW020423290526
45785CB00002B/697